ANY SIZE, ANYWHERE

EDIBLE

GARDENING

First published in 2012 by Cool Springs Press, an imprint of the Quayside Publishing Group, 400 First Avenue North, Suite 300, Minneapolis, Minnesota 55401.

© 2012 Cool Springs Press
Text and certain photography © 2012 William Moss

The information in this book is true and complete to the best of our knowledge. All recommendations are made without any guarantee on the part of the author or Publisher, who also disclaims any liability incurred in connection with the use of this data or specific details.

Cool Springs Press titles are also available at discounts in bulk quantity for industrial or sales-promotional use. For details write to Special Sales Manager at Cool Springs Press, 400 First Avenue North, Suite 300, Minneapolis, Minnesota 55401.

To find out more about our books, visit us online at www.coolspringspress.com.

Library of Congress Cataloging-in-Publication Data

Moss, William, 1970-
Any size, anywhere edible gardening : the no yard, no time, no problem way to grow your own food / William Moss.
p. cm.
No yard, no time, no problem way to grow your own food
ISBN 978-1-59186-508-7 (pbk. : alk. paper)
1. Vegetable gardening. 2. Container gardening. 3. Patio gardening. 4. Roof gardening. I. Title. II. Title: No yard, no time, no problem way to grow your own food.

SB324.4.M67 2012
635--dc23
                    2011045442

Project Manager: Billie Brownell
Design Manager: Brad Springer
Cover Design: Karl Laun
Interior Design: Diana Boger
Interior Layout: Heather Parlato
Production Manager: Hollie Kilroy

Printed in China

10 9 8 7 6 5 3 4 2

Dedication

This book is dedicated to everyone living in apartments, condos, townhomes, dorm rooms, or trailers as well as downsizers and newbies who all want to get out and grow!

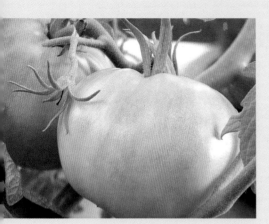

ANY SIZE, ANYWHERE
EDIBLE
GARDENING

THE NO YARD, NO TIME, NO PROBLEM WAY TO GROW YOUR OWN FOOD

WILLIAM MOSS

COOL
SPRINGS
PRESS

Growing Successful Gardeners™

MINNEAPOLIS, MINNESOTA

CONTENTS

Acknowledgments

My grandfather, James W. Moss, developed an inclination toward gardening in me by making me mow grass, rake leaves, cut hedges, and pick okra as a kid. I never thought I would garden for a living, but the seeds James sowed in my young mind finally began to sprout as an adult. I wish he were here today to share more of his wisdom and wisecracks.

Thanks to Roger Waynick for believing in me; may his spirit continue to watch over us all. My friends at Cool Springs Press also deserve thanks for their patience and understanding as I struggled through this project.

Indignantly, yet importantly, I must acknowledge rabbits, cold weather, and urban plots. Y'all toughened me up and helped me gain experience by tackling some tough problems. You guys are like the mini-bosses in Nintendo's Zelda games; once I got past you, I knew I was ready for anything. The rabbits' voracious appetites forced me to use raised beds and herbs to discourage them. Chicago's cold weather and short summer season made me learn how to grow more than just tomatoes and cucumbers. Especially relevant to this book, gardening in small urban plots taught me to become a more efficient and effective gardener.

Thanks to Momma for supporting me and allowing me to roam the woods as a kid. She deserves a big thank-you for not "whooping" me or freaking out when I brought home turtles, tortoises, lizards, snakes, crayfish, frogs, salamanders, and a host of bugs. The freedom and encouragement you gave me fostered my love of the outdoors. Oh yeah, and thanks for birthing me.

Adoration is given to my wife Natasha for loving me and having my back (and front too) at all times. You deserve a medal for putting up with this big old kid. Also, thanks for not calling Bellevue to come get me despite witnessing my rooftop gardening hobby slip into full-blown obsession. I could not have written this book without your support.

Preface

There's a special place in my heart for small spaces and community gardens. I grow crops and flowers in lots of places but James Park Community Gardens is unique. Surrounded by the good people (many decades older than I) there, I learned how to garden in small spaces at James Park before I had my rooftop, balcony, backyard, and other garden spots. That community garden is where I learned many important lessons.

The first year was a debacle. I planted the tomatoes late. Rank growth overwhelmed the too-small tomato cages and the tomatoes spilled over the ground. Between an early frost, pesky squirrels, nibbling voles, and gross slugs, we only harvested a few ripe tomatoes.

The ornamental section was worse. I built a berm (a raised mound of soil) to add structure and a focal point, then I promptly planted it wrong. I put the tall plants (cleome and cosmos) on the bottom and short plants (nasturtiums and marigolds) on the top. Soon I had an amorphous pile of plants with most of the flowers hidden under foliage.

But now I know tall plants should be planted on top of a berm and you plant tomatoes using big, sturdy staking systems as soon as the soil warms to about 60 degrees F. Many similar lessons were learned about other plants and veggies. Because of crop rotation and succession, the list of veggies we've grown in a community garden in that small plot is extensive. It includes tomatoes, sweet peppers, chilies, summer squashes, cucumbers, winter squashes, beans, peas, chard, beets, okra, lettuces, arugula, endive, spinach, tatsoi, pak choi, mustards, collards, broccoli, cauliflower, kale, asparagus, eggplants, fennel, carrots, parsnips, radishes, sunchokes, potatoes, sweet potatoes, onions, leeks, shallots, and corn. Whew!

Thanks for coming along as I share what I've learned and help get you started vegetable gardening.

Introduction

Welcome to you all! I'm excitedly writing this book to offer small space gardeners my expertise and encouragement. My first bit of advice? Release any trepidations or worries. Gardening should be *fun*. It takes skill, but growing plants is intuitive and as old as civilization. If prehistoric people could scratch out subsistence gardens using stone tools in some rocky dust, then *you* can grow a tomato successfully. And you can do it anywhere, from city to suburb and from farmland to container.

Be careful, this hobby is addictive. Greening can become obsessive. The desire to have living, green, ornamental, and healthy things in your presence is strong.

Gardening is almost instinctual and definitely beneficial. All the attributes of growing plants are too numerous and subjective to list here, but a few stand out. Gardening is mentally therapeutic and physically aerobic. Plants filter pollutants and particles from the air. Growing veggies saves money and provides nutrition. In cities, gardens soften the artificial landscape, buffer sound, and absorb stormwater. Plants provide habitat for birds, bees, and butterflies. Greening decorates and improves the look of any yard, patio, parkway, or balcony. In general, gardening is good for you, your family, and your community. With these benefits, neither the lack of space or time should deter anyone from gardening.

I live in a little apartment in one of the biggest metropolitan areas in the world filled with concrete and asphalt, yet I surround myself with plants and dig in the dirt nearly every day. I'd like to say I integrated gardening into my life, but honestly, it was probably the other way around. I've been blessed with opportunities to garden all across America from town to country in diverse settings, such as patios, rural yards, school grounds, church lots, botanic gardens, town squares, and municipal parks. However, the bulk of my experience was gained in my

three small space gardens: a residential backyard, a community garden, and a rooftop.

I dug my first hole in my ma's 30 × 30-foot backyard in a Chicago neighborhood. A couple years of success there and I had the itch. When you live in an apartment, there's only so much the landlord will let you do to the grounds. Fortunately, most cities rent plots at community gardens. Our roughly 30 × 16-foot space receives full sun, and we grow mostly veggies. But the necessity of having produce and flowers right outside my door forced me to expand again to the balcony and rooftop container gardens.

For years I did not think of my hobby-turned-profession-turned-passion as small space gardening. I knew it was a little different from landscaping an estate, but I did not think it deserved a separate category. Wrong! In hindsight there are tips, techniques, and suggestions that benefit small space gardeners in particular. Knowledge is half the battle.

If you are reading this, you probably fall into one of three categories. You have a small yard or maybe no yard. You are time-crunched. You are looking for expert tips and advice. In some cases it may be all three. It was for me when I started. Here are some words I wish I had read in those days:

1. **Have fun.** Gardening should be enjoyable. Fortunately, we're not subsistence farmers who depend upon garden crops for their livelihood. With supermarkets on every other corner, we don't *have* to harvest anything. Don't get me wrong; there's no vegetable you can buy at a store that can match homegrown. But it's not a matter of life or death. Enjoy yourself. Revel in the sunshine. Appreciate the butterflies, honeybees, ladybugs, and songbirds. Stay out in the rain to watch the changing sky and smell the fertile earth. If you are not finding enjoyment and relaxation in the garden—stop. Take a break and come back later.

2. **Don't stress.** I can't emphasize this enough. If you forget to water or have an insect infestation, it's *okay*. If your neighbor loses control of his riding lawn mower and demolishes your entire garden, it'll be *okay*. You can always plant again (on your neighbor's dime).

3. **Start small.** Don't grow more than you can weed weekly, and water often. There are so many delectable, nutritious, easy-to-grow veggies that you are going to want them *all* in your garden—go slow. There's nothing wrong with starting with a small plot or containers. You can expand later.

4. **Don't let a lack of knowledge intimidate you.** Every gardener was a novice once. And even for those who are seasoned gardeners, there are always new lessons to learn. This book was written to help you avoid some mistakes and succeed in the garden. Scores of plants and lots of dollars could have been spared had trial-and-error experimenting not been such a large part of my education.

Chapter 1

SMALL SPACE VEGGIE GARDENS: THE PERKS & GROUND RULES

SMALL SPACE GARDENING is *hot*. Any Internet search for the terms *container gardens*, *raised beds*, or *vertical gardening* turns up millions of results. In recent years it has been the fastest growing category of gardener. This segment of gardeners is composed of several groups. Urbanites represent a big part, as more people live in cities than ever before. Residents of cities and towns usually garden in small spaces by necessity. Others may have big yards but have limited time and/or energy. These include the time-crunched and downsizers who choose to cut down the size of their garden. New gardeners are other constituents of small-space gardening, and they often wisely start small to bolster chances of success and to keep from feeling overwhelmed.

Creative solutions to space limitations, like these modular grid boxes and plantable concrete blocks, can create a garden that is as much a conversation-starter as a high-yield food source.

Small Space Perks

While they often require more detailed planning, in some aspects small gardens can be easier. Garden design is less complicated. For instance, you may only have room for three tomato plants, but tending them will be much easier for you than the guy who is growing thirty. Maintenance is simpler. Weeding, tilling, amending the soil, fertilizing, mulching, and watering (except containers) all require less effort than in large spaces.

But less effort doesn't mean less vitality. Small spaces can have a big impact. Whether it's a simple hanging tomato on a porch or an intricate herb spiral mailbox planting, they all contribute to a better physical and social environment. Community gardens fill vacant lots with veggies and flowers. Raised beds bring color and interest to parkways and cul-de-sacs. Green roofs and wall gardens soften harsh cityscapes while freshening the air. Schools, churches, retirement homes, and hospitals use garden plots to recreate and educate. In this case, size does not matter. We may not have much space or time, but we won't let that stop us from planting flowers, growing food, and enjoying the outdoors. We can all "get out and grow."

One of my first gardens was a small piece of ground along the railroad tracks with a "Dead End" sign stuck in the middle (guerilla gardening isn't something new). I passed this weedy area every day on my way to work (I was a school teacher). I didn't know who owned the land, but I figured no one would make a fuss over its beautification. So I bought tools, plants, and mulch. I planted no edibles, just a few common ornamentals, such as wax begonias, cosmos, marigolds, and daylilies.

I didn't expect anyone to notice, but people did! Other train riders thanked me after work as I weeded the garden. When I lugged buckets of water from my apartment, neighbors told me how they enjoyed the cheerful flowers. Although I had seen these people for years, we'd never had a connection until that weedy patch of ground became a mini-garden that united us.

Why Grow Your Own Vegetables?

Few things are as beneficial and life changing as growing your own food. Vegetable gardening gets you outdoors, gives you some exercise, and provides you with healthy crops. Veggie gardens can give you both a sense of achievement and peace of mind.

Growing your own food is seeing a resurgence in popularity. It often is touted as a way to save money, but veggie gardening is not just about saving a few bucks. For instance, if you have an average growing season and harvest 5 pounds of sweet potatoes from a container planting, that's not a bonanza. You wouldn't get rich taking them to market, and it wouldn't cost you much to just go buy 5 pounds of sweet 'taters. But other factors add value to growing your own garden veggies.

First, homegrown produce is as fresh and local as you can get. Vitamins, minerals, antioxidants, and phytochemicals (beneficial plant chemicals) are at their peak when the veggie is picked. The quick trip to the kitchen means your body receives the most health benefits. Homegrown veggies are right outside your door. There's no need to drive to a supermarket to get veggies that have been transported from across the continent. If you are the impulsive type who gets a hankering for a fresh spinach-onion-tomato omelet at odd hours, grow the plants for 'em. They'll be right there whenever you want them.

Second, you control all the additives. If you don't want your family to ingest residues from pesticides, fungicides, herbicides, synthetic fertilizers, or preservatives, use techniques and products approved for organic gardening. I never push gardeners to be completely organic, but I recommend organic and sustainable practices whenever possible. A wide selection of pesticides and fertilizers approved for organic gardening is readily available. Labels can be misleading, so read the ingredients. And look for the Organic Materials Review Institute (OMRI) listing or United States Department of Agriculture (USDA) approval.

Another factor is variety. Supermarkets carry one or two types of each veggie. That's a sparse selection compared to the hundreds of varieties that exist. If you grow vegetables from seed (many are easy), your choices are nearly limitless. You can grow the usual varieties or rare, gourmet heirlooms with neat colors and complex flavors.

Plus, growing your own food is one of the most gratifying experiences a person can have. Ask gardeners about their best veggie crops and they'll start to smile. Prepare for a long, jovial conversation as they excitedly speak about the merits of their garden and harvest. Few gardeners really think they are self-sufficient, but it feels *good* to grow your own food.

So factoring in freshness, proximity, availability, organic growing methods, variety, and self-satisfaction greatly increases the value of the homegrown veggies. Only the gardener can put a monetary price on his or her garden's harvest. For many it's priceless, although they will happily share their bounty.

Recently I saw conventionally grown heirloom pumpkins for sale in upscale markets at $8 for 5 pounds. So how much would my organically grown 20- to 30-pound heirloom cheese pumpkins sell for? I don't know. But it would have taken a pretty penny to buy my well-tended pumpkins. However, I happily shared them with family and neighbors. That's another plus of homegrown veggies: they make great gifts.

Ripe & Ready

We grow vegetables as much for the satisfaction of harvesting as the nutrition. Something about picking crops makes us feel proud, confident, and humble. To go from tiny seed to ripe veggie is a miracle. We don't control the process. It is already programmed in the plant. We just help out along the way and get to reap the benefits. The sense of satisfaction is ageless. You smile whether it's your first harvest season or your fiftieth. It literally represents the fruits of your labor, and they are sweet.

Vegetable or Fruit?

For this book, a "veggie" will mean any home garden crop, including fruits. Technically, vegetables and fruits are different. Vegetables have edible roots, stems, and leaves. Fruits are fleshy structures containing seeds. Some of the less sweet, more savory fruits are grouped as veggies for culinary purposes. Tomato, pepper, squash, pumpkin, and cucumber are examples of *fruits* that are commonly referred to as vegetables.

TRUE VEGETABLES & THEIR PLANT PART

Roots	Stems (Bulbs & Tubers)	Leaves	
Carrot	Celery	Collards	
Parsnip	Onion	Kale	
Radish	Potato	Lettuce	
Sweet potato	Rhubarb	Spinach	

Small Space Veggie Garden Ground Rules

A few simple rules help promote good garden health and growth. To get the most out of a small space, understanding some techniques that prevent or limit diseases, waste, toxins, poor soils, and other problems is useful. This allows you to have a productive garden without a large yard.

Sustainability

Sustainability promotes methods and techniques that do not deplete resources or cause lasting harm to the environment. The tenets of sustainability—conserve, reduce, recycle, and reuse—fit *perfectly* with small space gardening. We conserve through techniques such as intercropping and mulching. We reduce the use and cost of resources through Best Management Practices. We recycle nutrients through composting and water with rain barrels and cisterns. And we reuse or repurpose materials (wood scraps, hangers, plastic flatware, string, plastic egg cartons, and so forth) in the garden rather than trash them.

There's a lot of flowery rhetoric and poetic waxing about sustainability, but basically it boils down to being efficient and economical. When I first started gardening, I took advice from my grandfather and other seasoned gardeners. The methods they showed me are the same ones that we now call sustainable. The old heads just called them common sense. These methods are not new. Altruistic reasons aside, you should practice sustainability because it's cheaper and it works.

How? You can use less water if you mulch. Your harvest will increase if you plant in succession. Making your own compost saves money and supplies the best soil amendment. By allowing proper spacing and providing healthy soil, you won't have to buy as many fungicides or pesticides.

Sometimes you will need chemicals in the garden. Avoid those that leave residual toxins to reduce negative effects on your local habitat. Residual toxins can kill beneficial wildlife in the garden, damage the surrounding environment, and harm our health. If chemicals are needed, look for those that are more gentle on the environment (OMRI and USDA listed).

Best Management Practices (BMP) are a specific set of commonsense guidelines that modern gardeners use to generate a bountiful harvest with a small footprint.

Best Management Practices

Best Management Practices (BMP) go hand in hand with sustainability. BMP were developed by professional gardeners and farmers. The practices stress cleanliness and preparation, which is essential in small spaces to limit the spread of disease and increase yield. BMP also promote the conservation of resources, which means conservation of money in your pocket. The techniques in this book follow Best Management Practices, some of which are listed in the Appendix.

Getting Started

Do a site analysis first. Inventory the sun/shade patterns, utility and power lines, existing trees, pathways, garages, and other structures. This is *crucial* information whether you're planning a large landscape or even a single container. The results will determine the gardening space, prep work required, and refine your gardening goals.

The location of underground utility lines is most important to in-ground gardens. Don't dig without knowing where they are. Hitting a gas line completely ruins your day. During the filming of a landscape makeover show at an Atlanta home, I hit the gas line with an auger. We had called to have the gas line marked, but apparently someone made a miscalculation. Once we realized what happened and smelled gas, I did my best Roadrunner impersonation and kicked up dust as I ran across the street. No one was hurt and the gas company came out to repair the line that afternoon. But we were done filming for the day. We were lucky it only cost us money and time.

If utility lines are overhead, your tree selection may be limited. You won't encounter this often when growing veggies, but later you might decide to grow ornamental and fruit trees. Pick varieties that will stop growing well short of any overhead lines. If a tree grows into the lines, call a professional to prune it out. In my younger, rasher, broker days, I chose to trim an apple tree from the power line myself. I foolishly climbed up the tree with a handsaw to remove the offending branches. From ground

Here's a typical yard, and the landscape features in it:

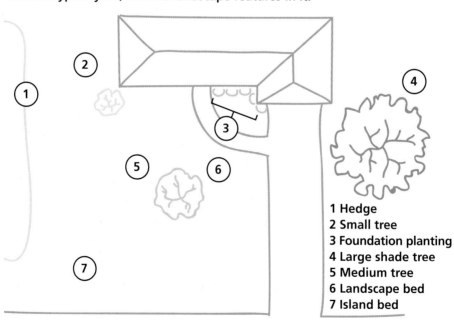

1 Hedge
2 Small tree
3 Foundation planting
4 Large shade tree
5 Medium tree
6 Landscape bed
7 Island bed

level it was impossible to tell they were tangled. After the first big branch was cut, it twisted and pulled the lines to the ground. Another ruined day, but, thankfully, no electrocution. The simple solution is to choose plants within the scale of all your space limitations: sideways, underground, and above.

Pathways, trees, garages, hardscapes, and utility boxes aren't dangerous, but they can affect your gardening success. Unless you can convince people to change their walking routes, never plant in pathways. Gardeners, particularly in community spaces, often try to redirect foot traffic with raised bed plantings or shrubs. But people are creatures of habit and will trod right over your barberries or kale, many times completely oblivious to your efforts. To avoid frustration, embrace the pathway and make it part of your design.

It's the same with all landscape elements. Trees and garages are a mixed blessing in veggie gardens. They protect plantings from strong winds and provide the sheltered habitat that most veggies want, but they also cast shade. Air-conditioning boxes are another mixed bag. You can't plant near them or the AC unit may be damaged. But you can build a protective trellis around your AC unit, which gives you a vertical element on which to grow climbing veggies like cucumber and peas. When you complete your site analysis, you'll have all the answers necessary to get started.

Sunlight & Growing Season

During your site analysis, make sure to note the location, amount, and duration of sunlight. It's good to know how much light your space receives, where it shines, and how that changes through the seasons. This helps you make a successful choice when buying plants.

Vegetable plants need *lots* of sunlight. Field greens are about the only crop that can grow in partial shade, and they won't be happy about it. Measure the amount (full, partial, filtered) and duration (number of hours) of summer sunlight in your space before choosing the location or plants for your veggie garden.

Most veggies would prefer eight or more hours of direct light. Other plants in your garden may be able to get by with less. Plants labeled for full sun exposure need six or more hours of unobstructed sunlight. Part sun plants require four to six hours. Part shade plants thrive in dappled light or two to four hours of sunlight. But there are plants that can handle the complete shade of tall buildings or evergreen trees. Unless your outdoor gardening space is on the dark side of the moon, you've probably got enough light to grow a garden.

Your geography determines the number of days in your growing season. In areas that have cold winters, your growing season is the number of days between the *last* frost in spring and the *first* frost of autumn. (Excessive heat and drought can also affect the growing season.) Colder areas, like Alaska, have a short growing season during summer. Hotter places, like Phoenix, also have a short growing season from late winter to spring (before temperatures become too hot to grow some veggies).

Short growing seasons will affect your crop selection. Casaba melons take 110 hot days to ripen. Minneapolis barely has 110 frost-free days, let alone hot ones. So Prince can't grow casabas in his backyard garden. Many potato varieties stop growing when temperatures are above 80 degrees F. In Phoenix, *nighttime* temps average over 80 degrees in July. So those in the Sunbelt have no chance of growing potatoes as a summer crop. But with a little tending and some planning, many crops will thrive in both cities. If you don't live in areas with extreme climates, you will probably have a growing season that's long enough for most veggies.

Healthy Soil = Healthy Plants

Soil is the foundation of vegetable gardening. Without good soil, you can't grow good veggies. The soil feeds and anchors plants. Building good soil pays big dividends when gardening. It is not a static solid, like concrete or a block of wood. At their best, garden soils are dynamic, fluid, and full of life. Plants get the vast majority of their requirements from the soil. A gardener's main job is to improve the quality of the growing medium beneath their feet. A well-drained, loose textured soil allows roots to absorb water, air, and nutrients. The bottom line: healthy soil grows healthy plants.

By the way, we will call the growing medium "soil" in this book. An old gardener taught me years ago that soil grows plants. Dirt is what is on the bottom of your shoe. Dirt is what's on your car after a long, snowy winter. Dirt is dirty and dead. Soil is vibrant and alive.

If you know or suspect the soil is contaminated with toxins (like some urban soils), take precautions, especially when growing veggies. Lay heavy-duty landscape fabric across the ground as a barrier. Construct raised beds at least 12 inches tall on top of the fabric. Line the inside of the bed with landscape fabric. Bring in uncontaminated topsoil or compost soil mix to fill the raised beds. Then you can confidently plant anything, including edibles. Or, just grow in containers.

Amending the Soil

Organic matter includes compost, aged animal manures, peat moss, humus, pine needles, straw, shredded leaves, and grass clippings. The types available depend on your region. Incorporate some into your garden soil because organic matter:

* improves the drainage of heavy soils
* improves the texture (tilth) of compacted or heavy clay soils
* increases water-holding capacity of sandy or rocky soils
* supplies nutrients and minerals as it breaks down
* buffers against pH problems

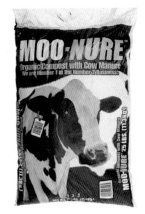

Soils that are rocky, gritty with sand, sticky with heavy clay, or stinky from being waterlogged need amending before planting veggies. You are trying to create a balanced soil that looks, smells, and feels rich.

Textbook garden soil consists of the following:

* 45 percent solids—minerals and crushed rocks that hold the nutrients
* 25 percent water—fills in the space between the solids and allows the nutrients to move toward the roots
* 25 percent air—this pore space keeps the soil loose and allows roots to absorb oxygen, which prevents root rot
* 5 percent organisms—fungi, bacteria, insects, animals, roots, and all their waste comprise the living part of soil

Don't get caught up on the percentages, just concentrate on improving what you've got. That means amending with organic matter. For all soil types, it is a magical panacea.

Till or dig generous amounts into the top 6 inches of soil. If you want a vigorous workout, incorporate organic matter to 12 inches deep. This is called double digging because it takes a lot of shoveling. Double digging builds your soil and character, so share the goodness. Invite your strong-backed friends to a soil amending party with a promise to return the favor.

Fortunately, double digging is a one-time thing. But, when growing veggies, you will still need to amend the top layer annually. Organic matter decomposes over time and your veggies' voracious hunger depletes the soil of nutrients. I amend in fall when the garden is going dormant. It's the easiest time because I'm cleaning up and digging holes to plant daffodils and tulips. But amending is not season sensitive. Anytime you can work the soil is a good time to amend.

Soil Test & pH

Taking a soil test helps determine what you have. Soil test kits are available in garden centers and at your local Agriculture Extension Service office.

(The Agriculture Extension Service is a nationwide network of departments, part of the USDA, that advises commercial farmers and home gardeners.) A simple soil test can tell you what nutrients are available or lacking in your soil. Knowing this makes it simpler to amend the soil for productive growth. A soil test will also indicate your pH level.

Soil pH measures the acidity (number of hydrogen ions, H^+) in the soil. The scale ranges from 1 (strongly acidic) to 14 (strongly basic). Fresh water is neutral at 7. People are familiar with acids and bases in their foods and beverages. Acids taste sour and astringent, like lemon juice, soft drinks, coffee, and vinegar. Bases are usually chalky-tasting and bitter, like milk, yogurt, beans, Brussels sprouts, and asparagus.

Most garden plants grow best at a pH of 6.8, but a range from 5.8 to 7.2 is acceptable. If the pH is too acidic (below 5.8) or basic (above 7.2), minerals can get "locked up" in the soil and will be unavailable to plant roots. This damages plant development and stunts growth. Veggies in soil with extreme pH values may not die, but they don't produce well either. Fortunately, plants are forgiving and pH values are adjustable.

Use a soil test or simple pH kit found in most garden centers to check the values. Adjusting the pH of the soil is similar to improving the texture and nutrients. You've got to incorporate amendments and you do it every year.

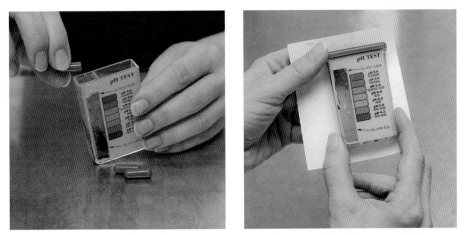

A pH test kit can be purchased in just about any garden center. The kits are simple to use but accurately reveal the level of acidity in your soil so you can make informed decisions when amending the soil.

Adding crushed limestone (calcite or dolomite) raises the pH of acidic soils. Spreading sulfur fertilizers lowers the pH.

Compost and other organic matter is once again the silver bullet. It acts as a buffer in all soils and helps plants deal with out-of-balance pH values. This is yet another reason to continually add organic amendments to your soil.

Selecting Plants & Seeds

Before buying veggies in pots or cell packs, inspect them thoroughly. Check the leaves for insects or disease. Choose healthy, stout plants with several sets of deep green leaves to give them the best start. Check to make sure each plant is securely anchored in the six-pack or pot, which indicates a well-established root system.

Some garden centers offer fruiting veggies in bloom and some may already have fruit forming; that's fine. In areas with short growing seasons, larger transplants mean faster and larger yields. However, when you transplant it into your garden, *remove* all flowers and fruit to help larger plants acclimate. If you don't, instead of focusing on establishing itself in its new home, the plant will put energy into flowering and fruiting. To get big, high-yielding veggies, a plant needs to fully establish and develop before switching its energy into fruiting.

Seeds are like tiny treasure chests. Each one is capable of producing a miracle. Sowing seeds is one of the most fundamental and rewarding pleasures in gardening. The journey from an inanimate speck of debris to a lush plant is an incredible process, even for the most grizzled veterans.

Germinating seeds can be a fun family activity. It's quality time together and the kids will learn valuable life lessons. Parents and teachers can use seed germination to teach kids the relationship between cause and effect, observation, measuring, and weather patterns. Plus, kids have fresh tendons and springy muscles made for stooping and bending.

General Rules for Starting Seeds

* Buy seeds with the current year's date stamped on the packet or use fresh seeds that you collected from the previous year's garden.

* Indoors, sow seeds in a loose potting soil mix. Some mixes are specifically made for germinating seeds. Outdoors, amend the soil and rake the surface smooth. A loose soil allows the first roots and shoots to easily sprout.

* Sow seeds in moist—not wet—soil mix. Seeds in wet soil have lower germination rates and higher instances of disease.

* Supply bright light. Not all seeds need light to germinate, but after sprouting most seedlings require four-plus hours of light for best development.

* Develop an ability to ruthlessly thin seedlings. This is a tough one. Fresh seeds usually sprout in overabundance. Without thinning, they will all struggle for their share of space and nutrients. The seed packet will detail thinning and appropriate spacing.

* Water the soil, not the leaves. Outdoors, use a nozzle with a gentle setting so the seedlings aren't washed away. Indoors, trays or pots should be placed in water so that seedlings are soaking water from the bottom up.

* Plant seedlings sown indoors in their outside space once they have three sets of leaves. Follow directions on the seed packet for spacing.

How to Work with Peat Pellets

Step 1: Peat pellets can be purchased in bulk at most garden centers. They are discs when purchased and when set in water to hydrate they expand within their netting container. Poke seed holes once the pellets have fully expanded.

Step 2: Plant seeds according to the directions on the packet and let them germinate under good growing conditions. Plant the peat pellets directly into the ground in your garden.

How to Start Seeds Indoors

Step 1: Fill the individual cells in a starter tray up to the top with loosely packed starter mix. Poke holes for the seeds spaced according to the seed pack recommendations.

Step 2: Plant your seeds in the seed holes.

Step 3: Water the soil to dampness only—do not overwater to the point that seeds can float out. Cover the tray to keep the moisture trapped.

Step 4: Check the starter tray occasionally for the first few days to test the moisture level and add water as needed. The tray should receive at least eight hours of light (from sunlight or grow lights) every day and be kept in relatively warm conditions.

Step 5: Carefully transplant the healthiest sprouts to larger pots (4 in. diameter, or bigger) so they can establish stronger root systems before you transplant them into your garden.

Seeds vs. Transplants

Many veggies are best grown from seed. Some, including carrots, peas, beans, and okra, develop taproots and should be sown directly in the garden. Other veggies can be started indoors and transplanted outside later. Starting seeds indoors gives you a head start on warm-weather veggies, such as tomatoes, peppers, and squash, which means a bigger harvest.

Compared to container-grown transplants, seeds are cheap and plentiful. You'll have more than enough for the current year. Sow about twice what you think you will need. Put the rest back in the packet and seal it shut with masking tape or a hard fold. For extra protection, place the packet inside a clean sandwich baggie. Store the excess seed in a cool, dark, dry place for use in future seasons, or donate to a school or community group.

Starting from seed keeps the garden cleaner. Lots of diseases, weeds, and pests enter the garden on the plants that you buy. Slugs, oxalis, and root rots are just some of the marauders that have used potted plants as Trojan horses to invade my gardens. Growing from seed limits the amount of unsterilized soil and plant material introduced to your space. Since you have more control, it is also easy to go organic and sustainable. Unlike with potted plants, you can determine all the variables with seeds.

Another huge advantage of planting with seeds over potted plants is that you get to start gardening much sooner. Seed catalogs make great winter reading. You get to peruse kaleidoscopic photos and dream of the coming season while icicles dangle from the tree branches and house eaves. Make sure your seeds arrive at least six weeks before the last spring frost.

Transplanting a sturdy plant that you've raised from a seedling can be a moment of great pride for a gardener.

To start seeds, use a germination soil mix. Pots, trays, takeout boxes, and even egg cartons can serve as seedling containers. Fill the container with *moistened* (but not wet) soil mix. Push the seeds into the top of the moist soil. Place a lid, cover, plastic wrap, or wax paper on top of the seed tray to maintain high humidity. Keep the soil moist and place in a very warm location, like on top of a refrigerator. Once the seedlings begin sprouting, remove the cover and place the tray in a bright, warm location. Keep the soil mix moist, not soaked, and avoid wetting the leaves. Rotate the tray every couple days to prevent seedlings from leaning toward the light.

Thin the seedlings according to the seed packet. When each has two sets of leaves, transplant the seedling to individual pots and fertilize with a half-strength water-soluble fertilizer.

Place in a bright space until warm weather arrives, then plant in the garden. Space the veggies according to instructions on the seed packet.

Placement & Spacing

Designing a veggie garden is simple. Everything is based on practicality. Rows should run north to south, but if you have to go east to west, it will be okay. The tallest plants are best positioned on the north side of the garden (at least in the Northern Hemisphere). This prevents shading of the shorter plants. Leave enough space between rows, blocks, or beds to walk, work, and water. I've damaged many a plant with a wayward water hose or misplaced step. Now I try to leave plenty of space amid plantings.

The spacing between individual plants is a controversial subject. Seed packets or plant tags give optimal spacing under ideal conditions. Many intensive, square foot gardeners ignore traditional spacing and cram as many plants as possible into an area. Kudos to the successful intensive gardeners, but I prefer a different approach.

Plants want their space just like people. Packing 'em in creates weaker plants that are more susceptible to disease and insects. Poor air circulation is a leading cause of fungal diseases. Some intensive gardeners recommend planting sixteen onions per square foot. Personal experience has shown me that nine per square foot will yield larger onions at about the same weight. If I were a subsistence farmer with the free time and dire need to work the garden constantly, maybe I would be a crammer too. As it is, I garden for enjoyment. I want to give my veggies a good start and allow them the proper space and time to produce crops.

Planting

Digging holes for plants always makes me smile. Planting feels like spring. It's a renewal of hope and another chance for life. The process is fairly straightforward for you but rough on the plant, even traumatic. Roots, the blood vessel of plants, are ripped apart. They're yanked from their home and plopped in a strange environment. It takes them awhile to adjust to the new conditions. While they are recovering from transplant shock, plants won't be 100 percent functional. Many of the roots are severed, so their ability to draw water is reduced. A few techniques can ease their pain.

Prepare the hole before planting and make sure the soil is loose and moist. Soak the plant in a bucket of water to moisten the rootball, gently tease out any circling roots, and plant it at the same depth it was previously growing. (Tomatoes are an exception and will be covered later.)

If possible, pick cloudy, cool, and/or drizzly days for planting, so there is less need for water. Soak the soil afterward to give the roots every chance to drink. Check often to make sure the soil is still moist. If the weather is hot and dry, you may need water every day for a week before the roots regrow and the plant stabilizes. If it is cool or it rains, you may not need to water at all.

Intercropping, Succession, & Scale

When growing veggies, interplanting is often called intercropping. Small space gardens are planted more densely to make efficient use of all resources. Intercropping and succession are valuable techniques to improve efficiency and productivity. Rather than putting different kinds of veggies in separate areas, intercropping groups different crops together. Care must be taken to ensure the plants do not compete for the same resources, particularly space and light. The most common example of intercropping is with what's termed the "Three Sisters": beans, squash, and corn. They occupy different spaces above ground and their roots systems are complementary below ground. These plants actually benefit from intercropping.

Succession planting encourages you to continually sow new crops in the same space. You can do this with different types of veggies or the same one. Either way, while the current crop is bearing, the next crop is already growing. An example of the techniques can be seen in the okra bed at my community garden.

Onions are planted in very early spring. As I harvest onions for use in late spring, okra seeds are sown in the empty holes. I'm careful to sow the okra seeds away from the shadow of the remaining onions. By the time okra is established, all the onions are harvested. In late summer, as okra begins to flower and fruit, I sow field greens (lettuce, arugula, mustard) underneath them. In autumn, after all the okra is harvested and the stems are cut down, the field greens are ready. They'll continue to produce fresh greens until winter. Through interplanting and succession planting, that garden bed produces a variety of crops all growing season.

You can also do succession planting with the same crop. Some vegetables mature all at once because their ripening time is fixed by nature. Determinate-type tomatoes, cauliflower, bush beans, and zucchini have been known to overwhelm kitchens with their heavy production. Unless you plan to donate, can, freeze, or host a large dinner, spreading your harvest over several weeks is a better option.

Instead of sowing a whole carrot patch or a packet of beans, take it in chunks. Sow a new section every three weeks to keep the patch productive well into winter. Similarly, rather than planting four 'San Marzano' tomatoes at once, plant them at one-week intervals over four weeks. Sowing successively prolongs the harvest season and makes it more manageable.

A small-space garden should be planted densely, with concentrated nutrients and good management practices compensating for the tightness of the planting patterns.

Scale is another factor to consider in small spaces. Because full-sized plants can overwhelm the space, use dwarf plants where possible. Since Ma's backyard is small, dwarf hemlock and weeping spruce were better choices than their larger relatives. The dwarf evergreens can serve as design focal points without dominating the yard. The same applies for veggies. On my rooftop, dwarf cucumbers, bush beans, and patio tomatoes grow successfully in containers, where normal-sized varieties would struggle or fail.

This is where it pays to do some research. Read the descriptions on packets and in catalogs carefully, so you have a good idea of how much space the plant needs. Plant selection makes a difference. Many veggies have been bred specifically for small spaces. Search out plants that have desirable traits and fit into your garden.

Watering

Water is the lifeblood of plants. Small space gardens take less time to water, but you may have to water more frequently, especially during summer. Hot air and sunshine quickly suck moisture from the soil and leaves. Evapotranspiration is the two-dollar word for the combined desiccating effects of evaporation and plant transpiration.

Here are a few tips to make watering more effective:

* Use your finger to check soil moisture. Put your finger in the soil up to the first knuckle. Take it out. If the soil on your finger is moist, you're fine. If it's dry, it's time to water.
* Water early in the morning. Dawn is best, but definitively before the heat of the day.
* Water thoroughly so it soaks deep into the root zone.
* Try to keep the leaves dry to limit fungal blights like powdery mildew.
* While you're letting the hose soak an area, use the time to monitor your plants, cut flowers, or harvest some produce.

Evapotranspiration is especially hard on containers and hanging baskets, which are exposed on all sides. In a sunny location, it is not

A drip irrigation hose dispenses water effortlessly and with only minimal loss to evaporation.

A hose sprayer is convenient and allows you to direct the water with precise efficiency.

uncommon for hanging baskets to need watering *twice* a day. Small pots fare no better. Even large containers may need watering every couple of days during the height of summer. Water until the potting mix is saturated and runs out of the pot. On balconies, use a tray bottom to catch excess water or your downstairs neighbors may fuss. (Trust me on this one.)

Plan for the summer heat. Proper irrigation keeps the garden and the gardener from struggling. In most cases a soaker hose attached to a timer is sufficient for small gardens. Programmable in-ground and drip irrigation systems allow precise watering, and some are made specifically for patio and balcony container gardens. They automatically handle your watering chores. Regardless of the option, think about irrigation as you plant so it is not a problem later.

Vacation Watering

Summer vacations are tough on gardens. I've lost many a plant to summer trips. You've got a few options. The most common is to ask a friend to water in your absence. With a programmable irrigation system, you can feel free to go on vacation without calling in favors. Or take the laissez-faire route. Pray for rain and enjoy your vacation. The garden will be fine (or not); and you can deal with the fallout when you get back. Remember, farmers markets are open, and planting (even a second time) is fun.

Fertilizers

Vegetables are *heavy* feeders. Successful gardeners make sure nutrients are available when the plants need them. That means preparing a rich, organic soil *before* planting and fertilizing while they're growing. Fertilizer can be amended into the soil, spread across the surface of the soil, or dissolved in water. Water-soluble fertilizers are poured around the base of a plant or sprayed on its leaves (foliar feeding).

Fertilizers contain essential nutrients for plant growth. Small space gardens *must* fertilize to maximize growth. This is especially true in containers and hanging baskets that often lose nutrients through water runoff. Fertilizers are available in dry granular and liquid forms. Some are fast acting to give an immediate boost. Others slowly release nutrients over time, thus providing a steady supply for several weeks.

Proper fertilization takes some planning. There are some definite dos and don'ts:

* Do fertilize regularly.
* Do follow directions closely for mixing and applying.
* Don't overfertilize—ever.
* Don't fertilize when plants are not actively growing.

Plant roots only absorb fertilizer when they are actively growing. Fast-acting, water-soluble fertilizers won't remain in the soil. If plant roots don't absorb them, the fertilizers will wash or leach away from the garden. That's a waste of resources and the opposite of sustainability. So don't fertilize near the end of the growing season or when the garden is dormant.

These rules are particularly important for patio, balcony, rooftop, and vertical gardeners. In these small spaces water runoff quickly leaves the

Granular fertilizers can be dispensed accurately in a small garden. The ability to put the fertilizer right where it is needed allows you to use more highly concentrated nutrients than you could apply when broadcasting, as you would in a large garden or field.

garden, goes down drains, and moves into the environment. In natural habitats, fertilizer runoff alters ecosystems, promotes invasive species, and creates dead zones in bodies of water. By following the fertilization rules, you boost your garden, save money, and protect your local wildlands.

Fertilizers have numbers on them listing the ratios of three nutrients: nitrogen (N), phosphorous (P), and potassium (K). The numbers are listed in the order N-P-K. The nutrients function differently within the plant.

* Nitrogen promotes leaf and stem growth.
* Phosphorous helps produce flowers and fruit.
* Potassium increases overall health and disease resistance.

The numbers tell the percent of the elements by weight. For instance, a 10-20-10 fertilizer is 10 percent nitrogen by weight, 20 percent phosphorous by weight, and 10 percent potassium by weight. A soil test will let you know what nutrients are present or lacking, so you can make adjustments. (You wouldn't test container potting mix because it's not soil to begin with, but you can expect to feed container plants regularly.)

The most commonly used fertilizers are the synthetic granular forms. They are inexpensive, easy to transport, and easy to spread by machine or gloved hand. Since many synthetic fertilizers are water soluble, you can apply them as you water to kill two birds with one stone. Add the fertilizer solution at the end of your watering, or wait and fertilize the day after watering.

Organic fertilizers differ from synthetics. They are slow acting and generally not soluble in water, so they don't leach from your garden. This makes them more sustainable and appropriate for organic gardening. Organic fertilizers (such as worm castings, greensand, wood ash, recycled food scraps, bat guano, and so forth) are amended into the soil or spread across the surface, like topdressing.

Organic matter, such as manure and compost, has low but balanced amounts of all soil minerals and nutrients. It is heavy and more difficult to spread, but typically less expensive than organic fertilizers. Use organic matter like a topdressing or mulch. Amending with organic matter and slow-release fertilizers builds a healthy soil environment, where beneficial bacteria, earthworms, and good insects can thrive and fight the bad guys.

COMMON FERTILIZERS FOR VEGGIE GARDENING

Fertilizer	Nutrients	Water Soluble	Slow-Release	How Applied
Balanced granular	N-P-K in equal ratio	Yes	No	Soil amendment, water, foliar feeding
Compost	N-P-K-Ca in small amounts	No	Yes	Soil amendment, topdressing
Balanced organic	N-P-K	No	Yes	Soil amendment, topdressing
Organic topdressing	N-K with more nitrogen	No	Yes	Soil amendment, topdressing
Bone meal	N-P with more phosphorous	No	Yes	Soil amendment
Potash	K	No	Yes	Soil amendment
Ammonium sulfate (lowers pH)	N	Yes	No	Soil amendment, water
Dolomite lime (raises pH)	Ca	No	Yes	Soil amendment
Fish emulsion	N-P-K with more nitrogen	Yes	No	Water, foliar feeding

Good soil makes healthy vegetables, which in turn make healthy gardeners. The chart above reviews some types of fertilizer. Soil amendments are tilled or dug into the soil. Topdressings are spread loosely across the soil surface. Mulch is layered 2 to 3 inches deep across the surface. Granular fertilizer is dissolved in water, then poured around the root zone or sprayed on leaves.

Composting

Compost is decomposed organic matter. Rather than discarding plant waste, composting allows us to recycle our garden debris and kitchen scraps into nutrient-rich, loose, well-drained organic soil amendments.

Plant material is "eaten" by bacteria, earthworms, pill bugs, and millipedes. They all work together to transform dead plant tissues back into the building blocks of life.

Materials suitable for composting include garden and kitchen debris, such as leaves, stems, spent flowers, grass clippings, straw, cornhusks, peelings, rinds, apple cores, and so forth. Hard or fibrous materials, such as cornstalks, nutshells, and rinds, should be chopped into smaller pieces to speed decomposition. Avoid using wooden branches, bones, animal fat (including cheeses), and fresh animal droppings. These decompose slowly and can attract unwanted pests. Do *not* use diseased plants either.

Managing your compost consists of adding plant matter, keeping it moist, and turning the pile. Stirring a couple times a week keeps the pile well ventilated, which speeds up decomposition and reduces odors. A stagnant pile takes a long time to make compost and it can smell terrible. Aerobic bacteria quickly break down plant matter but need oxygen (supplied by turning the pile).

Many small, unobtrusive composting units are available for the small space gardener. Rotating compost bins take up more space but accelerate the process. If you have no outside space, you can still compost. There

A compost pile can be as simple as an out-of-the-way heap of organic matter that you poke at with a pitchfork from time to time. But the invaluable result is what gardeners call "black gold."

are undersink units for kitchen scraps. Vermiculture kits, which use red wriggler worms, are the most efficient and produce compost the fastest.

Composting provides gardeners with the best soil amendment *for free*.

Going from kitchen scraps and plant debris to prized compost can take anywhere from a few weeks to a few months, depending on temperature, moisture, and how often you turn the pile. Finished compost will look loose, rich, and woodsy. It can then be worked into the top layer of soil or spread across the ground like mulch.

Mulching

Mulching is one of *the* most beneficial things you can do for your garden soil. It retains moisture, helps moderate soil temperatures, suppresses weeds, and slowly releases nutrients. Veggies need a 2-inch layer of mulch throughout their growing season. Timing is critical when mulching veggies. Cool-season crops, such as broccoli and cabbage, should be mulched as soon as they are established, or a couple weeks after planting to keep the roots cool. Warm-season crops, such as tomatoes and squash, should not be mulched until the weather is hot. This gives the soil a chance to warm up, which warms the roots and increases growth and production.

Wood chips and shredded bark are typical types of mulch. They are available bagged or loose. Loose wood chips are sold by the yard (about a wheelbarrow full). Pine needles, straw, and grass clippings are other options. Mulching with 2 inches of compost, rotted manure, leaf mold, or other organic amendment combines all the benefits of mulch with a slow-release organic fertilizer.

Crop Rotation

George Washington Carver developed crop rotation methods to prevent nutrient-depleted soils. Planting the same crop in the same plot every year can lead to nutrient deficiencies in the soil, as well as disease and insect problems. Carver noted that plants from different families use different nutrients and are susceptible to different pests.

Rotating plots among different plant families helps reduce soil deficiencies and pest infestations.

Here's an example of a simple three-crop rotation plan involving plants from separate families: tomato (Nightshade family), bean (Bean family), and okra (Mallow family). In year four, you'll start over again.

	Year 1	Year 2	Year 3	Year 4
Plot 1	Tomato	Bean	Okra	Tomato
Plot 2	Bean	Okra	Tomato	Bean
Plot 3	Okra	Tomato	Bean	Okra

Weeding

Weeds take light, water, nutrients, and space from garden plants. If left unchecked, weeds can completely overwhelm a space. Their presence reduces the beauty and productivity of the garden. Weeds also attract and provide cover for pests, such as grasshoppers and aphids.

The definition of a weed is subjective, but any plant that is out of place or out of control can be weedy. In small gardens, *lots* of plants can be weeds. If a plant grows in the wrong area and is upsetting the intent and integrity of your garden, then feel free both to call and treat it like a weed.

Small spaces are easier to weed. The exception is community gardens. Because it's a communal site, there are a lot of common weeds. In nearly all gardens, wind and animals drop new weeds seeds in the garden throughout the year. It takes diligence to keep them down. Once veggies are established, mulch heavily (2 to 3 inches) to inhibit weed growth. Thick, lush foliage from some veggies, such as carrots and sweet potatoes, also discourage weeds.

Other plants need more help. Although not practical in a large garden, small spaces can inhibit weeds with a mulch and weed cloth combination. Here's how: clear the garden of visible weeds. Lay the weed cloth over the garden and stake it in the ground with landscape pins or spikes. You can cut holes for planting or seeding. Add a 2-inch layer of mulch on top of the weed cloth. Take care not to cover your plants or seeds. This combination of deterrents prevents more weed growth than either would alone in my community plot. But even in the best systems, some weeds will get through.

That's when you need some tool help. The CobraHead® is the best weeding tool I have ever used. Lately, though, I have been using the hoe more. It's gentle on the back and perfect for plants arranged in rows or grids. A hoe does really well in tight spaces. You can reach deep into the plants without stepping into the garden bed. Plus, a hoe is agile enough to be moved between plants and quickly chop down a swath of weeds.

Tools make weeding quick, but sometimes gloves are all you need. After a long day, hand weeding can be relaxing, almost therapeutic. I sit on my garden cart, put on some gloves, and rest my mind as my fingers move throughout the garden. They seem to instinctively know when and how to lift the crown of crabgrass or pull the taproot of dandelion.

Because hand weeding has become intuitive, my mind is free. Some of my most creative thoughts and plans can bubble up to consciousness. It's a time to dream of the future and reflect on the past. After weeding, the garden and I are both in better shape.

Pest Management

Healthy plants have fewer problems. Provide ample sun, good soil, and ample moisture while following Best Management Practices to keep plants healthy and resistant. After prevention, monitoring is the most crucial part of any pest management program. Take time to check your plants when you water and harvest. This is easier in a small garden because you literally have less ground to cover. Pests like to hide themselves and their eggs under the leaves, so be sure to turn them over for a look.

Good cultural practices are the best defense against fungal diseases, such as powdery mildew and blackspot. These include watering in the morning, giving plants the proper spacing for adequate air circulation, rotating crops every year, and keeping your tools clean.

When you find pests or diseases, mechanical methods are the first line of defense. Handpicking, crushing, washing off, and vacuuming off are initial efforts. The next step is biological warfare. Beneficial insects and bacteria are available to fight against bad pests. Ladybugs, tiny wasps, praying mantises, and lacewings seek out and eat bad bugs. Beneficial bacteria, such as B.t. (*Bacillus thuringiensis*), can stop most chewing insect pests.

When pests or diseases reach infestation level, chemicals may be necessary. OMRI- or USDA-listed products are contact killers and will not leave any toxic residues to harm pollinators, beneficial wildlife, or you. This is especially important for gardens where kids visit. Recent studies have shown that pesticide residues ingested by kids are linked to ADHD.

Monitoring allows you to identify and solve problems early. Make a mental note or actual chart when you first notice pests or diseases.

The information you record on the chart should be general observations. You don't have to count each individual bug or damaged leaf. But rough numbers will help you identify the disease or pest. The more information you have for your search the better. Check with plant information services at botanic gardens and extension offices and they will be able to help you better with this type of info.

Examples of pest and disease problems include leaf damage from chewing insects and root damage from nematodes, which are microscopic wormlike organisms that live in the soil.

PEST MANAGEMENT

Symptoms	Date	Date	Date	Date
Plant				
Overall vigor and health				
Color of leaves				
Insect pest description				
Number of pests on top of leaves				
Number of pests under leaves				
Pattern of leaf damage				
Area of leaf damage				
Percentage of leaves with disease				
Percentage of dead leaves				
Disease				
Treatment applied				

Wildlife Ecology

Small spaces can have a big impact on the local wildlife. Gardens are like islands in the middle of deserts, literally an oasis where birds and butterflies can rest and refill their tanks. Ecologically, gardens provide food and habitat to a host of animals. In cities they are essential sanctuaries for butterflies, songbirds, honeybees, dragonflies, and other wildlife that could not survive in human environments without a garden or green space.

The insects are usually the first wildlife visitors. On my rooftop nectar-rich plants bring butterflies and bees. Colorful flowers and culinary herbs attract honeybees and bumblebees by the dozens. Because they pollinate my veggies, bees are my favorite guests. As the container garden gets bigger and better, I see more types. Native green bees, sweat bees, carpenter bees, and even friendly wasps frequently visit.

Other than bees, other kinds of insects and creepy-crawlies are growing in number too. Spiders (orb-weaving, wolf, and jumping types) are the most prominent creatures. They are welcome anytime. From the looks of their webs, they kill hundreds of Lake Michigan midges and mosquitoes every day. Ants are nearly as common. I do not mind the tiny ones, but the large ones are a bit bold. I had a chance to get rid of the big queen ant. I saw her when she first flew in like a small biplane, but I was so impressed with her size and ability to find my small garden that I let her stay. Her offspring are everywhere now, but other than crawling on your legs, they do no harm.

Some beneficial insects that just stop by for a visit include dragonflies, stoneflies, ladybugs, assassin bugs, and lightning bugs. The lightning bugs are a new arrival. Apparently they showed up so their young could feast on my burgeoning population of slugs. That's the drawback to a wet spring and mulched containers. I would have never thought slugs would live in my windy, exposed, rooftop container garden, but habitat is habitat. Fortunately, they seem content to feed on fallen debris and have not damaged any of my veggies.

Of course, aphids, cabbage moths, June bugs, mosquitoes, and other prey species have to be present for the beneficial predators to arrive. A functional food web resides in and around the containers on my small rooftop. With that much life in such an inhospitable place, you can only imagine the amount of creatures present in a community garden or backyard. If you plant it, they will come.

There are many beneficial insects to welcome into your garden, such as the garden spiders and pollinating bees.

Chapter 2

TYPES OF SMALL SPACE GARDENS

SMALL SPACE GARDENING IS A SUBJECTIVE term. It can range from a single hanging basket with a chili pepper, to a backyard loaded with spring bulbs and summer tomatoes or a community plot filled with beans. The variations are endless, but they all offer the gardener a chance to work the dirt and grow.

Yards

Backyards and side yards are the most common place for gardens. They are usually the biggest section of ground space on the property, which makes them the best suited to grow crops. Most backyards also offer a little privacy and are exempt from homeowner association rules. This is in direct contrast with front yards, which are often viewed as a community façade, if not a communal property. It is common for associations to exclude veggie growing in the front and insist that all plantings be flowery and neat. But where it is allowed, I have seen spectacular front yard veggie gardens that really make a statement. To protest the wastefulness of lawns, some hard-core gardeners replace all their turf with veggies.

Before you go veggie garden crazy and rip out your grass, answer a few questions. Do the kids, dogs, or anything else need a patch of lawn on which to play? According to your site analysis, which yard is the most suitable? How are your neighbors going to react? What do you want to grow? This will give you an idea of what's possible in your yards.

Patios, Balconies, & Rooftops

Patios are common in urban areas. Decks are more popular in the suburbs. Neither has ground area, but both are suitable for container growing. Growing space is usually limited, though, as people use decks and patios for living. Decks with railings have more options because you can grow vertically on the balusters.

Balconies and rooftops have challenges that other areas don't face, like wind. On my rooftop there is a constant breeze, and the gusts are much more powerful than those at ground level—strong enough to damage plants and topple containers. On fully exposed areas, place containers in a sheltered spot (maybe against a wall) and protect the plants with wire cages and trellises. Wind also affects watering. A dry southwestern breeze can suck all the moisture out of large pots in a few hours. Containers may require daily watering during the hottest, driest times of the year.

Heat is another factor to consider. Patios, balconies, and rooftops are typically hotter than other parts of a building. Urban roofs (blacktop and reflective) are notorious for their scorching summer temps. Containers literally roast from radiant and convective heat. In some urban areas, the stifling heat—combined with hot, dry weather—creates desertlike conditions with high rates of water loss through evapotranspiration (evaporation plus plant transpiration).

Large containers handle adverse conditions the best. First, they are heavy enough to withstand wind gusts. The increased soil volume means more moisture-holding capacity, which means less water stress for the plants. Large containers also allow for individually contained gardens. Bulbs, annuals, perennials, veggies, and even shrubs can be combined for multiseason interest.

Community Gardens

Community gardens have been around for centuries. My English neighbor calls a community garden an "allotment." They are common in Europe and have a rich history here. Community gardens were wildly popular in America during World War I and World War II. At least 20 million people tended community gardens during World War II. About *40 percent* of all the veggies consumed in America were grown in these Victory Gardens in the 1940s. We may not make it back to those numbers, but community gardens are still a great way to grow nutritious food, promote self-reliance, and beautify the local area.

Like parks, most community gardens are public green spaces owned and operated by local municipalities. (Locate your nearest community garden at the American Community Gardening Association website: http://communitygarden.org). Rules and regulations differ across the

country, but typically there is a registration process for participants. My community garden charges a nominal fee for administration and water usage. Upkeep and weeding are the gardeners' responsibility or pleasure, depending on your perspective.

For years when my wife and I lived in a small apartment, my community garden was my only outdoor sanctuary. Community gardens give people without yards a chance to work the soil. We grow our food there, but the peace of mind and community they offer are just as important. Sitting on a bench chatting with my neighbor under my witch hazel, surrounded by daffodils and columbines, feeds my soul as much as the spring greens feed my body.

Some apartment complexes are acknowledging the need for garden space. Included with the rental space is a raised bed on the grounds. This would have been a dream for me. It provides apartment dwellers with produce right outside their door.

THE BENEFITS OF COMMUNITY GARDENS

* Provide food and nutrition to the community.
* Filter and purify the air and water in the community, especially important in urban areas.
* Provide habitat for local wildlife like birds, rabbits, and butterflies.
* Beautify the community.
* Allow for social interaction within a community. Gardeners help other gardeners. Community gardens also promote intergenerational interactions.
* Provide a location for social activities like gardening demos, harvest parties, and potlucks.
* Remove carbon dioxide and other greenhouse gases from the air (they are sometimes called *carbon sinks*).
* Provide opportunities to exercise and engage in physical activity.
* Keep the community active, which encourages social interaction and deters crime.

Sustainability & Courtesy in Community Gardens

The community garden I am part of decided to go organic because none of us wanted to bring produce with toxic chemical residues home to our families. All community gardeners should adhere to the same sustainable practices because of their close proximity and chemical drift. It is just a common courtesy.

Decide among yourselves what practices and products are allowed. Make sure it is well known by all gardeners because an unknowing person can contaminate the whole place. It only requires one application of toxic chemicals from one person on a windy day to remove the organic label from an entire community garden.

You should be considerate with plant choices too. Don't grow weedy, invasive, or overwhelming plants. Sunchokes are a native sunflower grown for their edible tubers. My great-grandmother grew them, so I wanted to try. Not only do sunchokes grow 8 feet tall and cast shade on neighboring gardens, but their underground roots travel across pathways and into other plots. This large, rampant, impossible-to-eradicate, neighbor-angering plant should never be grown in a community plot. (Sorry guys.)

Pumpkins, which can spread 20 to 30 feet in all directions, are another no-no. One year I grew gourmet cheese pumpkins and they spread into the adjacent plots of all my neighbors and their neighbors. Fortunately, they all like me, so instead of hacking out the vine, they pushed it to the side. The cheese pumpkins were prolific. They produced dozens of pumpkins that I gladly passed around to make up for the encroachment.

Take caution with your flowers too. Asters and goldenrods bring in many pollinators for late-season crops, but they are heavy seeders. Because their seeds spread by the wind and will definitely end up in other people's plot, they should also be excluded. Community gardeners have to be thoughtful of their neighbors in their selections. Aggressive, spreading plants are best planted in large gardens and farms.

Raised Beds

Deep, well-drained soil is not possible everywhere. In southern Florida, a layer of limestone rock is often only inches below the soil. In parts of Texas, the hardpan (caliche) makes good drainage impossible. Urban soils may be contaminated or completely paved over. Raised beds offer a solution to these problems.

I've built raised beds to improve drainage, provide ample root room, and limit contaminants, but the main reason I garden in raised beds is convenience. They are easier to manage. You add the soil-compost mix of your choice. There's no worry about contamination or missing nutrients. Because you bring in a good clean soil mix, there are no weed seeds and therefore less weeding.

Gardeners with achy backs and tired bones will find them easier. You don't have to bend or stoop as much to garden in a raised bed. Harvesting is a snap because the crops are higher. Your knees will thank you. After a few seasons of growing in raised beds, you'll wonder why you didn't get some sooner.

Wood, plastic composites, and cinder blocks are some of the common materials used to make raised beds. You don't have to be a carpenter to

construct them. Kits are available with all the materials you would need. If you ever played with Lincoln Logs™ or Legos™ or alphabet blocks, you can build a raised bed.

Many companies supply raised bed kits, one of which is Greenland Gardener™. It offers modular kits so you can build horizontally and vertically. They are surprisingly easy to assemble. My four-year-old nephew (T.J.) and I built two 8 x 4-foot and two 4 x 4-foot beds last spring. Most of them were one layer (8 inches) tall, but we built two layers for the 'Yukon Gold' potatoes, tatsoi, and 'Black Krim' tomato.

We were done in short time. T.J. still wanted to use the mallet. He wasn't ready for the project to be done. My plan was to tucker him out building the beds. Instead, we finished fast and he was still full of energy. I was impressed at how quickly the beds went up, but I had hoped to tire him out a little more to avoid playing Mario Kart all night.

We put 60 bags of organic planting mix in the Greenland Gardener beds. All the veggies grew well to my surprise. I expected the beets, okra, and other deep-rooted veggies to struggle in the 8-inch layer, but they grew like gangbusters. The 16-inch layer proved to be an even bigger surprise because it kept out rabbits. That alone makes me praise the kit. (Rabbits and I have a long history of conflict.)

When placing beds, allow enough room between them to comfortably walk without tripping or damaging the plants. Don't place raised beds too near alleys or streets where they can be damaged by an errant car or snowplow. Site the bed in a sunny location, fill it with a good compost soil mix, and you're ready to plant.

Container Gardening

If you don't have room for a garden plot or raised bed, you can *always* find space for containers. More people live in cities than ever. They move into apartments, retirement communities, and townhomes without much ground space but plenty of room for containers.

Container growing is not as productive as in the ground, but if it is only 50 percent productive that's much better than 0 percent. While a 16-inch pot is sufficient to grow most veggies, in this case, bigger is better. Get as large a pot as you can handle. Durability is another important factor. Digging in amendments and lifting out root crops could chip or break fragile pots. Freezing and thawing cycles can crack or damage fragile containers too.

Plastic composites provide a solution. They can take a hit, and plastic expands and contracts without breaking. Currently, plastic composites are the best material for veggie gardens because they are tough and ornamental. They come in a variety of styles and colors to mimic ceramic, stone, and wooden barrels. These are not your grand-mother's old, faded plastic pots. You'll also have your choice of sizes and shapes to fit any patios, balconies, porches, rooftops, entrance-ways, decks, or windowsills.

Plastic pots with a wide opening are the container of choice for vegetable gardening. They don't let moisture transpire through the container walls and they can withstand impacts and temperature fluctuations. These peas sure seem happy in their plastic pot, don't they?

If this is your first time growing veggies in containers, choose the biggest pot that you can safely handle. Remember that it weighs much more with wet soil inside. You can test the weight in the garden center by putting soil bags inside and lifting. If it's too heavy, choose a smaller one. Container mobility affects your gardening enjoyment and your back. Also, those of us with balconies, decks, back porches, and rooftops must be conscious of weight limits.

Don't get me wrong, I have all types of containers and nothing is more beautiful than a well-planted ceramic container garden. But for my veggies, plastic containers are easiest. In October, when I have to move my tomatoes from their sunny, exposed spot to a more sheltered location to avoid frost, I'm thankful for lightweight plastics. A 20-inch stone container of tomatoes is essentially immobile, and immobility significantly shortens the growing season for container veggies in colder climates. The goal is to get a big container and keep it as light as possible.

To help lighten large containers filled with soil, use container inserts. Several of my planters are over 2 feet tall, but tomatoes need only about 8 inches of soil depth. The large containers make a bold design statement, but I don't need 2 feet of soil. By using container inserts, which take up space, you lessen the amount of soil mix needed. Anything that reduces container weight and spares my back (two fewer 50-pound bags of soil to carry up four flights of stairs) is welcome. There are several options.

Ups-A-Daisy® is a plastic circle that fits inside planters and acts as a fake bottom. Ups-A-Daisy comes in various sizes to fit any pot. Better Than Rocks™ is a recycled plastic material that resembles a mesh filter. Better Than Rocks is cut to size and placed in the bottom of containers. You can use as many layers as you want. My largest containers have five layers or about 5 inches of Better Than Rocks on the bottom. Packing peanuts are another common option. Regardless of your choice, container inserts are a big help in reducing the overall weight of the container.

Creating Container Gardens

Before filling the containers, place inserts in the bottom to reduce the amount of soil mix needed. Inserts also reduce the weight of a finished container. Packaged potting mixes are the best choice for growing media. Using soil dug from the ground in containers is never ideal. Packaged potting mixes are lightweight, moisture retentive, pH balanced, and well aerated. Plus they do not harbor any fungi, bacteria, insects, or weed seeds that would cause problems later.

Finally, the plants selected should have a stern constitution. The largest container with the best potting mix will fail if the wrong plants are chosen. Know your climate. If you are in an extremely arid environment, choose drought-tolerant plants. If you are on the coast and receive sea spray, pick salt-tolerant plants. If you are in the far north and expect early frosts, select cold-hardy plants. But don't fret—choosing plants is the fun part. Hundreds of plants thrive on my harsh, exposed, windy rooftop. I've had failures but many more successes. The challenge has given me a new appreciation for plants and their will to live.

For gardeners without yards or community plots, container gardening gives us a taste of that All-American dream of a backyard garden. We can go outside and enjoy sitting by a green oasis with herbs, veggies, and flowers. Like any gardening endeavor, start small. Plant a few containers to feel your way and see what works best for your particular site and taste. In a short time you will have decorative containers brimming with edibles (or flowers or foliage). Remember, it is a learning process with occasional setbacks, but all in all container gardening is a great way to green your space and your life.

Window Boxes

Some people have no flat space for a garden or a container. For them window boxes may be the only option to grow outdoors at home. Window boxes make a bold statement wherever they are used. I've seen them decorate the front façade of mini-mansions in suburbs of Oklahoma City and produce a bounty of veggies on a brownstone in the Bronx.

For those in buildings, check with your association and/or superintendent to make sure you meet all codes before installing a window box. Because most window boxes (and rail troughs) are long and shallow, they dry out quickly. A moisture-retentive soil mix can mean the difference between watering every day or watering twice a week.

When it comes to placing window boxes, accessibility, not light exposure, is the most important factor. If you have to put the box on a shady side, you can find plants that will grow happily. But if your box is hard to reach or water, you won't be successful. Also, out of sight, out of mind. That window box of purple basil in the second bedroom might look great from the street, but if you always enter through the garage and rarely visit the second bedroom, that planting is in trouble. More plants die in window boxes than anywhere else. Place them where they are within easy reach and improve the view (both indoors and out).

Vertical Gardening

Vertical gardening has been a popular technique for dealing with small spaces since at least the Hanging Gardens of Babylon. Vertical space is often overlooked (pun intended), but adding vertical elements in small spaces greatly increases the growing area. Besides providing more space for veggies, vertical gardens can also soften walls and fences, screen unsightly views, and provide shade. Cages, strings, poles, stakes, chain-

link fences, and hanging baskets offer simple ways to grow up. Trellises, pergolas, and wall garden units are more complicated versions on the vertical theme.

Trellises, Pergolas, & Arbors

Trellises, typically made from interwoven latticework, are either freestanding or attached to a wall. They are *perfect* for small spaces. Trellises provide support for weak-stemmed plants and small vines, such as tomatoes and summer squashes. Arbors are large, freestanding structures with a canopy for shade. Pergolas are a type of extended arbor that can be freestanding or attached to a building. Pergolas often follow pathways and have a canopy of latticework. Arbors (including pergolas) can support heavy vines, like pumpkins have, and large hanging baskets. In small spaces, arbors are the defining hardscapes and are typically placed in courtyards, parks, and school gardens.

Hanging Baskets

Hanging baskets may be the most popular form of vertical gardening. Seems like everyone's grandma had a basket of impatiens hanging on the porch. But today, grandma might have a tomato hanging from it. Hanging baskets can be placed on balconies, decks, and other places where it is impossible to grow in the ground. As long as there is light and a place for a hook, you can hang a plant. The basic design is available in many styles and purposes. They range from ornate baskets for colorful annuals to inexpensive grow bags for veggies.

Whether you have a wire basket with begonias or a Topsy Turvy® with tomatoes, hanging pots will require more watering and fertilizing. During hot, dry spells, you may need to water twice a day. A moisture-retentive potting soil mix helps, but since the basket is exposed on all sides, water loss through evapotranspiration is extremely high.

I travel often so watering every day is not possible. However, I was able to grow a successful Topsy Turvy basket recently with marjoram and chili peppers (the Italian variety 'Corni di Toro'). Because both are tough and drought tolerant, I could miss a day or a weekend without them turning to toast. My hanging tomato was not so lucky. After one missed day of watering in July, it was crispy and *dead*. Maintenance and plant selection are the keys to growing successful hanging baskets.

Green Walls

Green or living walls are fast becoming popular, especially in urban areas where growing space is limited and walls are plentiful. Green walls can be freestanding or attached. Plants can grow up from the ground to cover a wall or units can be mounted on a wall to hold plants. Vines with suction cups and/or aerial roots are suited for this. Although they're experiencing a resurgence, green walls are not new. At many of our universities, ivy creeps upward to form lush, green walls.

Wall units allow other types plants to grow vertically. They consist of shallow pockets filled with soil or some other light-growing media. Most are modular so you can start small and expand later. When installing a wall unit, secure it sturdily because after planting and watering, they will be much heavier.

Although not suitable for most veggies, wall units can grow other edible plants. If you want herbs but don't want to take away ground space from your veggies, then attach a wall unit in a sunny spot. You may have to water more than usual, depending on exposure. If you can't water regularly, choose shorter, small-leaved plants, like thyme and oregano.

Green walls can be installed inside too. Indoors, a green wall serves as living art and purifies the air. Indoor air is often more polluted than outdoor air, especially in office buildings. Volatile organic compounds (VOCs) found in carpet, paint, plywood, computer components, toner cartridges, nail polish, hairspray, cleaning products, and so forth have negative effects on health. Use spider plants, dumb canes,

flamingo flowers, ferns, and so forth for indoor wall units. The tropical plants act as Mother Nature's biofilters by removing toxins and releasing pure oxygen. Whether in an office with tropicals or on a patio with herbs, green walls add decorum and vibrancy.

Outdoors, their aesthetic, environmental, and economical benefits are similar to green roofs and include the following:

* Provide green space to a barren area
* Screen and soften buildings and other cityscapes
* Insulate buildings against cold and hot outdoor temperatures
* Purify the air by removing pollutants and particles
* Absorb and filter stormwater
* Serve as habitat for beneficial wildlife, such as butterflies, honeybees, and ladybugs

Vertical Vegetables

Growing *up* may be the only way small space gardeners can grow some veggies. Fortunately, many veggies can climb and actually benefit from being off the ground. Some are ramblers, like tomatoes, that have to be continually tied to a support as they grow. Others, like cucumbers and peas, attach themselves.

The benefits to growing veggies vertically include the following:

* You can plant more veggies per square foot of soil for intensive gardening.
* Growing vegetables vertically allows good air circulation to keep leaves dry and prevent fungal diseases.
* It prevents soil from washing onto leaves and spreading disease.
* It makes veggies easier to monitor and harvest.
* It's a cleaner harvest. It also keeps dirt and slugs off veggies.

Selection is important when growing veggies vertically. Choose smaller varieties. Many pumpkins and winter squash will grow too large on a trellis. Heavy fruits might break the vine and the trellis. Instead, plant a climbing summer squash variety or lighter crops like pole beans.

Trailers & Cascaders

Not all plants are suited for hanging baskets. The complete exposure, quick-draining soil, and limited root room make it a difficult environment for most plants. Resilient plants that cascade over the side are ideal for hanging baskets, green walls, and window boxes. Dwarf or bush types with smaller fruits are more successful. For instance, cherry and plum tomatoes produce well in hanging baskets, while the larger tomatoes, like indeterminate beefsteaks, can fall off or break the vine altogether.

Drought-tolerant, aromatic herbs are some of the easiest plants for vertical gardening. Hyssop, marjoram, and creeping rosemary can grow as tough ornamental trailers and can be harvested all season long. With proper selection, vertical gardening space can grow healthy, productive plants.

VERTICAL PLANTS

Many plants are adapted to climb or cascade. Vines are the most common climbers. Their methods for climbing include twining, tendrils, aerial roots, suction cups, and rambling. Vines that twine or have tendrils attach themselves to supports. They readily climb chain-link fences, trellises, strings, and poles without much help from you. Those with aerial roots and suction cups will also independently climb, but they need solid surfaces like brick walls or wooden fences. Ramblers have no special methods of climbing. Gardeners must attach these weak-stemmed plants to supports or they'll just flop across the ground.

Vines

Vines are decorative plants that can take tough conditions. Many will grow happily in shaded areas, whether from trees or a neighboring building. Some popular ones are listed in the following chart. (Some ornamentals are listed here to demonstrate their method of climbing.)

Climbing Away

Vine	Attribute	Light	Height
Grape	Fruit	Sun to part sun	16 ft.
Clematis	Flowers	Sun to part shade	8–20 ft.
Carolina jasmine	Fragrant flowers	Sun to part shade	20 ft.
Japanese hydrangea vine	Foliage and flowers	Sun to part shade	40 ft.
Boston ivy	Foliage	Sun to shade	60 ft.
Morning glory	Flowers	Sun to part sun	20 ft.
Pole beans	Fruit	Full sun	10 ft.
Squash	Fruit	Full sun	8 ft.
Pumpkin	Fruit	Full sun	20 ft.
Nasturtium	Edible foliage, flowers	Sun to part sun	10 ft.

Climbs By	Structure	Time to Maturity
Tendrils	Arbor	4-plus years
Twining	Trellis, arbor, chain-link fence	2-plus years
Twining	Trellis, arbor, chain-link fence	4-plus years
Aerial roots	Wall or solid fence	10-plus years
Suction cups	Wall or solid fence	10-plus years
Twining	Trellis, chain-link fence	1 summer
Twining	Trellis, chain-link fence, poles, strings	1 summer
Tendrils	Trellis, chain-link fence, poles, strings, cages	1 summer
Tendrils	Arbor, chain-link fence	1 summer
Rambling	Trellis, chain-link fence	1 summer

Chapter 3

TIME-SAVING TIPS

TIME-CRUNCHED HAS BECOME a common description of modern life. Our days are filled with activities, commitments, necessities, and distractions in a way that was unimaginable a couple generations ago. Everyone from toddlers to seniors has their schedules packed with events and tasks that in the moment seem absolutely crucial to their existence. Small pieces of plastic and metal interrupt our routines and summon us to work, chat, watch, and tweet at all hours of the day and night. The peaceful evenings and weekend mornings spent lounging on the porch with family and neighbors are as endangered as sea turtles. We feel compelled to stay busy. The time-crunched want to garden, but it has to fit within their hectic lives.

Downsizers are typically older gardeners who no longer have the inclination, time, or energy to tend large spaces. They may have tended a large backyard veggie patch in the past, but now they prefer a raised bed by the side door. They don't want to give up gardening. They are just done working a large space. I've watched this time and time again. At 79 my grandfather parked his tractor for the last time. At 88 my great aunt stopped her decades-long fight against the honeysuckle vine that threatened her fig tree and veggie patch. At 84 my friend Tom gave up his community plot. They still wanted to garden, but the rigors were just too much.

In small spaces you can grow veggies without much time or effort. It takes planning, organization, and an acceptance of the limitations. If you garden in a raised bed two hours a week, you are not going to harvest as many tomatoes as the guy down the street who works in his backyard garden two hours a day. But that's okay; you may not need or want that many tomatoes. In the following paragraphs are some tips to save time and energy while gardening.

Mulch

Whether you are growing kale or pecan trees, nothing is as beneficial as proper mulching. You won't need to water or weed as often. Using rich compost as mulch reduces time spent fertilizing too.

Mulch is important for limiting transpiration and keeping your investment in precious water to a minimum. Shredded wood is a popular and widely available mulch option, but many gardeners prefer compost or other topdressings that have a more neutral effect on the soil nitrogen balance than decomposing wood products.

Amend Soil with Organic Matter

Another tip to reduce watering time is to amend with organic matter. Compost, worm castings, rotted manures, and so forth build the water-holding capacity of the soil while maintaining good drainage.

Install Irrigation Systems

Watering the garden is the most frequent and time-consuming task. Let technology do it. Install a timer on your spigot and use a drip line, soaker hose, or sprinkler.

Drip lines work in the ground and in containers. Holes in the line leak water precisely where you want it. Soaker hoses are more general and not suited for containers. Place soaker hoses under mulch, while drip irrigation lies on top.

Sprinklers are common; however, overhead watering may invite fungal diseases. Also, most oscillating sprinklers were made for large yards and can be awkward or impractical to use in a small space. When I use the oscillating sprinkler at the community plot, my neighbors' gardens get as much water as mine.

You *probably* won't need as many hoses as this example from my community garden demonstrates, but a water faucet with multiple connections will allow you to run several hoses throughout your garden.

Whichever you choose, put the system on a timer and watering takes care of itself. Set it for one hour or more every two or three days, depending on your climate. You want to soak really deep into the root zone. Program it to finish as you are leaving in the morning so you can check to see if the plants received the right amount of moisture. If you are in a rainy or dry spell, adjust the timer accordingly.

Make Your Own Self-Watering Pot

Containers can dry out fast. In the height of summer, you may need to spend an hour a day watering a container garden. Changing the drainage helps reduce watering. Look for containers that do not have predrilled drainage holes. Instead of putting holes in the bottom, make them on the sides of the pot.

You will need a drill, a $^1/_4$-inch bit (or smaller) to start the hole, and a $^5/_8$-inch bit (or larger) for the final hole. Big pots need six holes all around at about 3 inches up from the bottom. For smaller pots, four holes placed 2 inches up will do. With the holes on the side, water can sit in the bottom. This acts like a reservoir that the roots can access when they need it. The holes allow excess water to drain out and air to come in. The containers are more drought resistant and you can gain one to two days between watering with these drainage holes. On my rooftop container garden where I have more than 150 containers, this reduced watering from a seven-plus-hours-a-week task down to three hours. (Yet somehow I get no more rest than before. But I appreciate another way to spend less time holding a water hose.)

Grow Low-Maintenance Crops

If your goal is to save time and energy, don't grow crops that require tending or harvesting every day. Indeterminate tomatoes need continual staking, pinching, and cleaning. Okra, lettuce, green beans, and zucchini need frequent harvesting to produce at their peak. At some point during their growth cycle, these veggies are going to demand some time.

SAVE TIME, WATER, AND EFFORT

Once I had over fifty pots on my rooftop garden, I knew normal watering wasn't going to cut it anymore. I watched in anguish as water that I had carried upstairs in 5-gallon buckets (*heavy* water) leaked out the bottoms of the pots and down the drain. Sometimes when potting mix in containers is dry, it becomes what's called "hydrophobic" and repels moisture. The water will run down the cracked soil along the sides and right out the drainage holes. It was a waste of effort, water, and time, all of which are resources too precious to squander.

My other problem with watering was that I was often gone filming television shows for Discovery or HGTV. While two-week shoots in summer might be fun for me, they were rough on my container plants. Lots of veggies and flowers died while many of the survivors were so dry, the potting mix became hydrophobic and required extra watering just to get wet. I spent hours upon my return watering, just trying to save a few tomatoes and asters.

Large saucers to hold water under the containers did not help. During the heat of summer, the water quickly evaporated from the saucers. Very large and deep saucers did hold water longer, but that led to stinky, stagnant water, which bred mosquitoes. I tried water bags, which are canvas bags full of water with tiny holes on the bottom. But the size of the bag needed for an extended stay would have taken up all the space in the containers. Wine bottles did not offer a solution either. (This seems counterintuitive, because wine inside a bottle is often a solution to many problems.) I had plenty of wine bottles to fill with water and place into the pots, but the science is tricky. You need the mix to clog the opening and keep the water inside the bottle when you turn it upside down in the container. But if the soil is packed too loosely, the water runs out too fast. If the soil is too compact, water won't leak out at all. There had to be a better way.

The solution? When I made my own self-watering containers, things got easier. Now, during regular watering and especially before long trips, I saturate the containers. With a supply of water at the bottom of the pot, plants can better survive long absences. The mix retains more moisture and is less likely to become hydrophobic. Watering is easier and more efficient. Using this tip to make your own self-watering pot saves water, effort, and time. Plus, you'll get to use power tools.

Conversely, potatoes, onions, peppers, and sweet potatoes can take care of themselves. Put these root crops in the right conditions and they'll grow. Occasional weeding, watering, and fertilizing are all they ask. There is no urgency to harvest. The crop will be waiting on you when you have time to stop by.

Grow in Raised Beds

Gardening is easier in raised beds. You add good soil mix, so there is no tilling or double digging. A layer of landscape fabric underneath stops weeds from growing through. Any weeds that blow in are easy to remove in the loose soil. Because the area is raised, working in the bed is kinder on the joints and tendons. At harvest time the veggies are easier to see and reach.

You don't have to be a carpenter to build raised beds. There are kits available that you can assemble in less than 30 minutes. Some of them are modular, so you can expand upward and outward if you choose. This could have kept my grandfather growing beans and peppers for a few more years.

Grow Resistant Crops

Fighting diseases takes up a lot of time and resources. If the disease kills the veggie, then all the time spent planting and tending it will have been wasted. (Or more positively, deposited in the experience bank. How's that for cognitive dissidence?)

Do yourself a favor and select resistant varieties of veggies. This doesn't mean you won't have diseases, but it gives you the best chance to avoid common problems. Disease-resistant varieties are usually highly productive too.

Pick Prolific Plants

As well as growing resistant crops, if you have a limited amount of time, select plants that will give you the most reward. There are a few things more frustrating than tending a non-productive veggie. Growing 'Mr. Stripey' tomatoes is a good example. This sweet beefsteak tomato has orange and red skin with orange and red flesh. 'Mr. Stripey' is a joy for the eyes and the taste buds. However, it is not that prolific, and it ripens very late. Despite growing them in rich soil in raised beds, my sister Teresa, who lives in South Carolina, only got *two* tomatoes off her two plants. I was fortunate to harvest five from my container-grown 'Mr. Stripey'. Teresa works twelve-hour shifts and struggles to squeeze in gardening here and there under the merciless southern sun. She vowed to never again grow 'Mr. Stripey'. She says her efforts are better spent on 'Sunset's Red Horizon', 'Mortgage Lifter', and the prolific 'Gardener's Delight'. For the time-crunched, planting veggies that are disease resistant *and* productive are your best bets.

Chapter 4

HOW TO GROW VEGGIE ALL-STARS

THE BEST PERFORMING plants for small spaces are generally compact or have easily controlled growth but also offer lots of bang for your buck. To get you started, these are my favorites.

My veggie all-stars list covers some of the most commonly grown vegetables. Grains (corn, rice, oats, wheat) are large space crops, so they were omitted. There are many other tasty veggies (asparagus, eggplant, leeks, pumpkin, beet, sunchoke, spinach, chard) that we didn't literally or figuratively have room for in this small space gardening book.

These descriptions are designed to help the gardener have success. These include general growing rules, but you know there are exceptions to every rule. Certain varieties may have different characteristics or habits. The list is not all encompassing, but these are some of the healthiest, easiest to grow veggies, and they perform well in small spaces.

BEANS
BUSH, POLE, STRING
(Bean family)

* **Culture:** well-drained, deep soil; medium moisture; provide supports
* **Yield:** 2 pounds per planting; ½ to 2 pounds per square foot
* **Mature Plant Size:** 2 to 10 feet tall
* **Where:** large containers, trellises, fences, railings, poles
* **Ripens:** 8 to 12 weeks after planting

Beans are a protein-packed warm-weather veggie on an annual vine or weak-stemmed plant. They are one of the most productive crops you can grow in a home garden. Beans are often used in crop rotation plans because they nourish the soil by transferring nitrogen from the air to the soil, thereby improving fertility for the next crop. Because they grow well vertically, beans are easy to work into most gardens.

 Look for bush varieties to save space and time in the garden. For instance, 'Royal Burgundy' only grows a couple of feet tall, excels in containers, and produces over a long season with little maintenance.

How to Select

Beans come in two main types—pole and bush. Both types have scores of varieties in different colors, sizes, and shapes. Bush types have a determinate growth pattern and develop their beans in flushes. The taller types take a little longer to develop, but they produce beans steadily throughout their season.

Pole beans require a lot of height and considerable staking to poles or trellises. Between the two types, pole beans generally produce a larger crop over a longer period. But if they're well watered and maintained, bush types are nearly as productive.

How to Plant & Maintain

Bean seeds sprout fairly quickly and are one of the best crops for children to learn about germination. Plant in mid- to late spring when the soil is warming. Space and thin according to seed packet instructions.

Use a balanced fertilizer when planting. Add an organic topdressing or other slow-release fertilizer before planting and four weeks after planting. Beans need regular watering, especially during hot, dry weather. Consistent moisture when

they begin flowering greatly increases the yield. Mulch with compost in early summer to conserve moisture and suppress weeds.

Beans need support. Even bush types can benefit from staking or caging. Pole beans can grow over 10 feet, so gardeners often tie long bamboo canes together to form bean teepees. The teepees are more decorative and sturdier than a single row of poles. Pinch the tips of the growing stems when pole bean vines are 5 feet long to keep the pods within reach.

Harvesting

Beans provide a couple options for harvesting, depending on how you want to use them.

Harvest	Preparation	Pod Edible	Long-Term Storage	Pod Size
Young	Raw; cooked	Yes	Blanched, then frozen; pickled	Tiny and short
Fully ripe	Cooked	No	Dry	Larger and longer

Bean pods are only edible when they're harvested before the seeds fully form. The entire pod can be eaten raw. Check to make sure the pods are smooth with no protruding bumps. For most varieties, that's when the pods are between 3 to 6 inches long or a few days after the flower opens. Some wax bean pods remain tender even at 8 to 10 inches long. The best way to know if the pods are still edible and tender is to pick one that represents the average and take a bite. If it's crisp and sweet, you got there in time.

Once the beans inside begin to swell, pods become tough and inedible. They can be picked, shelled, and cooked at this point. Some gardeners leave them on the plant for the next stage of ripeness. When they're fully ripe,

the pods become leathery and dry. The seeds are completely developed, hard, and sometimes colorful. These dried beans can be cooked or stored indefinitely in a cool, dark, dry place.

I prefer to harvest pods when they are still tender and use them in salads and stir-fries. This means harvesting every 2 to 3 days during the peak of the season. My neighbors at the community garden can't get to their plot that often, so they use their beans for winter soups. They let all the pods completely ripen and pick them off the withered vines.

The benefits of waiting for pods to mature are that you only harvest once and it's easy to store the dried beans for later use. However, there are drawbacks to this method. The pods are inedible, you can't prepare them like fresh green beans (no stir-fries, no salads), and overall plant production is less than it is with plants you continually harvest for fresh beans.

Because I can spend more time in the garden, I'm biased toward harvesting beans young when everything is edible. With such small spaces I need to maximize production. But it's cool that beans provide the time-crunched with a simple harvest option.

Eating

I grew up eating lots of beans. My grandfather would bring bags of beans from his garden and my momma and I would either snap beans in summer or shell the beans in autumn. At that time we called them "string beans" because there was a tough fiber running down the seam. That fibrous "string" has been bred out of most varieties now. Still, string bean remains a common term synonymous with green and snap beans.

My mother invariably boiled them whether they were shelled or not. I avoided all beans for *years* after I left for college. As I got older, I appreciated them again. Although shelled beans are tasty, they can't compare to fresh beans. Green beans enliven all dishes. I even like them boiled now, especially with new potatoes.

CARROTS & PARSNIPS
(Carrot family)

* **Culture:** loose, deep soil (amend with sand); medium moisture
* **Yield:** 2 to 4 pounds per square foot
* **Mature Plant Size:** 18 inches tall x 18 inches wide
* **Where:** raised beds, and in large, deep containers
* **Ripens:** carrots, 8 to 12 weeks after sowing;
    parsnips, 14 to 18 weeks after sowing

Carrots are a favorite of Bugs Bunny and that's really the only rec-ommendation needed. Besides that, both these hardy crops have health benefits. Carrots are loaded with Vitamin A, and parsnips have Vitamin E. With their ferny foliage, both are attractive in the garden and resemble their cousin, the wildflower Queen Anne's lace. In fact, if not harvested, they flower profusely in late spring with beautiful white blooms that attract crowds of beneficial pollinators.

Finger and ball carrots only need a depth of 6 inches of loose soil, which means they grow well in containers. They also ripen the quickest, which is an asset in any small-sized garden.

Selecting Plants

Carrots come in white, yellow, purple, and the familiar orange. They also vary in size, which can determine their best growing conditions. Carrots are classified as long, medium, short, finger, or ball-shaped. Long carrots are the standard market variety and store the longest. The shorter types are a better choice for shallow or rough soils. Select carrots fewer than 6 inches long, like ball-shaped and finger types, for container gardens.

Common parsnip varieties have large roots, often over 12 inches long and 4 inches wide. They need deep soil and are not suited for most containers.

How to Plant & Maintain

Prepare a loose, deep, fertile soil in an open space for carrots and parsnips. Amend with organic matter, slow-release fertilizer, and sand.

A loose textured soil yields straight, smooth taproots. Rocks, roots, and other obstacles cause carrots to grow misshapen and twisted.

Plant carrot and parsnip seeds when the soil temps begin to warm in mid-spring. Their seed does not store well, so the packet you purchase should be marked with the current year's packed-for date. The seeds are very tiny. Sow sparingly to avoid lots of thinning. Before thinning the seedlings, water them so they're easier to pull out. Water again after thinning to help disturbed roots heal. Eat thinnings in salads or as use as a garnish.

Succession planting works well for carrots. Sow some seeds every three weeks from mid-spring through early summer. This will provide carrots from midsummer through winter. With the right varieties, you can have garden-fresh carrots six or more months of the year.

Keep the soil moist. Dry soil can lead to carrots splitting. Spread organic topdressing over the area when plants are 6 inches tall. Mulch with compost to conserve moisture and suppress weeds. Interplant with onions to discourage pests.

Harvesting

Harvest carrots when they are small; a 2-inch diameter ensures that they are sweet and tender. Pull or dig them carefully to avoid breaking or damaging the taproot. Cut the tops and tiny roots before bringing inside. Carrots will store about two weeks in the refrigerator.

Parsnips need winter cold to become sweet and nutty flavored. Leave them in the ground through cold weather. In late autumn, mulch heavily or place hay bales on top of them to make winter harvesting easier.

Carrots that ripen in autumn can also remain in the ground until they're harvested. The advantage is easy storage in perfect conditions, especially in warmer areas. But in cold areas the disadvantages of frozen ground and freezing temps make it a tough call. The other storage option for cold climate gardeners is to dig carrots in late autumn and remove the tops along with any small roots. Then place them in boxes of sand in an unheated garage or shed.

If you overwinter carrots and parsnips, dig them all out as soon as you can in very early spring. Otherwise, they'll quickly become tough and woody as they prepare to flower.

Eating

Homegrown carrots don't have to be peeled. Just wash them thoroughly to remove soil, roots, and grit. The best raw carrots are the tender finger varieties. They flavor and sweeten salads. Cooking seems to enhance the sweetness. My great-grandmother used to make a tasty dish of tangy marinated carrots and onions for Christmas dinner; I can taste it now. The dish was spicy, salty, and sour as if it were a vinegar marinade. Too bad I never got the recipe. You can't go wrong if you eat carrots raw or roast them with meat.

COLE CROPS
BROCCOLI, BRUSSELS SPROUTS, CABBAGE, CAULIFLOWER, COLLARDS, KALE, KOHLRABI
(Mustard family)

* **Culture:** fertile soil; above average water especially during hot, dry weather
* **Yield:** broccoli, Brussels sprouts, cauliflower, kale, kohlrabi, 1 to 2 pounds per plant; cabbage, collards, 1 to 4 pounds per plant
* **Mature Plant Size:** broccoli and Brussels sprouts, 36 inches tall x 24 inches wide; cabbage and cauliflower, 12 inches tall x 18 inches wide; collards and kale, 24 inches tall x 36 inches wide; kohlrabi, 12 inches tall x 12 inches wide
* **Where:** raised beds, and in large, deep containers
* **Ripens:** kale and kohlrabi, 8 weeks; broccoli, cabbage, cauliflower, collards, 12 to 20 weeks; Brussels sprouts, 26 to 30 weeks

This plant family contains many superfoods. The vitamins, minerals, cancer-fighting phytochemicals, and antioxidants are why I started eating broccoli as an adult. Once I grew these vegetables in my garden and ate them fresh, I realized they were not only healthy but tasty too. Now, "taking your vitamins" is rather tasty.

 Cole crops have shallow root systems, meaning they grow well in containers. Decorative varieties of kale, such as 'Russian Red', do double duty, adorning dinner plates and gardens from early spring to late fall.

Selecting Plants

The broccoli clan is composed mostly of cool-weather crops. Selection will depend upon your tastes, climate, and space. For instance, Brussels sprouts are a good crop, but they take up space for a long time before they produce. In the time and space it takes to grow one Brussels sprout plant, you can grow a spring crop of six kohlrabis, a summer crop of 'Roma' tomatoes, and a fall crop of kale. Nothing against Brussels sprouts, but intensive, small space gardeners may not want to allot the space to one plant for that long.

Climate also is a consideration. Collards are the best at taking hot, long summers. Brussels sprouts are the hardiest in cold. Cauliflower is the most cold sensitive. Climate won't preclude you from growing any of them (unless you live in tropical areas), but you'll have better success if you plan the best matches.

All varieties of all types in the broccoli family are available as seeds. Garden centers will occasionally have a few varieties for sale as transplants, which will save you a week or two on harvest time.

How to Plant & Maintain

Broccoli and its siblings require well-drained, fertile soil, but do not till or dig the soil before planting. They prefer firm ground. Direct sow seeds into the garden or plant transplants. Thin and space according to the seed packet's instructions. Start in mid-spring for summer and autumn crops or late summer for winter and spring crops. Protect seedlings and young plants from frost.

Plastic buckets with their bottoms cut out can easily (and inexpensively) be used for different sorts of protection. Position a bucket over a seedling if bugs are attacking the young plants or if you think a late cold snap will damage your cole crop seedlings.

Add slow-release fertilizer to the soil before planting. Use a balanced fertilizer at planting and again six weeks later. Two weeks after planting, add an organic topdressing, then mulch with compost. The mulch keeps the soil temperatures cooler during hot weather.

Water regularly, especially during dry periods, even in winter. Overwintered collards, kale, broccoli, cabbage, and Brussels sprouts may need water if rain has been below average.

In windy areas broccoli and Brussels sprouts will need staking to prevent damage. Wind stunts the growth of most cole crops, so shelter them as best you can. On rooftop and balcony gardens, place containers against a wall or railing for extra protection.

Young Brussels sprouts.

Harvesting

Cut broccoli when the buds are still tight. If the buds are loose and flowers are beginning to open, you've waited too long. Harvesting the top broccoli head will promote side shoots that you can cut for several more weeks. (The side shoots will not be as large as the first head.) Harvest regularly to promote production of more side shoots or broccoli will stop producing.

Cauliflower, like broccoli, should be harvested while the buds are still tight. Unlike broccoli, cauliflower rarely forms side shoots and can be composted after harvesting.

Kale and collards have the longest harvest seasons. If you need a lot, cut the whole plant; otherwise, harvest individual leaves from the bottom up. Both kale and collards taste sweeter if they have gone through a frost.

Top – Red Express cabbage; bottom left – Russian Red kale; bottom right – Kohlrabi.

During warm weather put the leaves in the refrigerator for a few days to help "sweeten" them. Remove the tough veins and midribs before cooking.

For cabbage and kohlrabi, take the whole plant. Cabbages can resprout from the cut stem and develop several smaller heads. Remove the outer leaves from a cabbage head and the swollen stem of kohlrabi. In the refrigerator cabbage will store for at least six weeks. Kohlrabi only lasts about a week.

Brussels sprouts develop from the bottom up. Harvest the lower sprouts when they are still tight. If the leaves begin to open, the flavor

COLE CROPS

Nearly everything on all cole crops is edible. However, if you take too many leaves from broccoli plants for greens, you'll have fewer florets to harvest. You can also eat young cauliflower leaves. But since kale and cabbage produce more leaves and require less preparation, they are better choices for greens.

Edible Parts	Leaves	Leaf Buds	Stems	Flower Buds
Broccoli	Yes*^	-	Yes*	Yes
Brussels Sprouts	Yes*^	Yes	No	Yes*
Cabbage	Yes	-	No	Yes*
Cauliflower	Yes*^	-	Yes*	Yes
Collards	Yes	-	No	Yes*
Kale	Yes	-	Yes*	Yes*
Kohlrabi	Yes*	-	Yes	Yes*

* - not the main crop

^ - require lots of cooking to tenderize

is reduced. Once it begins to bud, harvest frequently and the plant will continue to produce sprouts for about eight weeks. Without frequent harvesting, the plant will stop sprout production. A touch of frost sweetens the sprouts.

Eating

Although the plants in the *Brassica* genus are siblings, those leaves, stems, leaf buds, and flower buds are very different in the kitchen. Fresh cauliflower and broccoli are delectable raw. As a general rule, steaming and stir-frying retain all the vitamins and beneficial compounds. Some gradeners will want to cook them longer even if some nutrients are sacrificed. Collards, in particular, need a lot of boiling and a side of chow-chow relish to make it onto my plate.

CUCUMBERS & SUMMER SQUASHES

(Squash family)

* **Culture:** deep, rich soil; space for air circulation; above average water
* **Yield:** 12 to 20 fruits or 3 to 5 pounds per plant
* **Mature Plant Size:** bush types, 3 feet x 3 feet; vine types, 6 feet x 2 feet
* **Where:** raised beds, large deep containers, trellises, fences, railings, poles
* **Ripens:** 10 to 12 weeks from sowing seed

Cucumbers, squash, and zucchini are closely related warm-season crops. All love the summer heat and produce prolifically. Their fruits contain Vitamin C and *lots* of moisture. The high water content is what makes cucumbers cool and crisp. Squash and zucchini fruits have creamy, mild flesh—especially if they're harvested while still small and tender.

 Most cucumbers and some squash ('Tromboncino' and 'Cucuzzi') can be trained to grow upwards to use available vertical space. If you don't have vertical supports, look for bush types like 'Salad Bush' cucumber and '8 Ball' zucchini.

Selecting Plants

Cucumbers and summer squash have several growth habits. Large bushy plants require large gardens. Trailing plants cover a lot of ground but will grow vertically and can be trained to a trellis. Compact bush varieties are best for containers or small spaces.

Pickling and slicing are the two types of cucumbers. They have different tastes and are harvested differently. Decide how you want to use cucumbers before selecting a variety. Summer squashes are available in many types, including yellow crookneck, yellow straightneck, scallop, and zucchini. The differences are mainly in size, with scallops growing on the smallest plants with the smallest, sweetest fruit. Zucchinis or marrows are at the other end with large plants and big fruit.

All varieties of all types are available as seeds. Garden centers will occasionally have a few varieties for sale in pots. Potted plants transplanted to

Nothing says a trellis has to be unattractive! Cucumbers usually spread out on the ground, but in a small space garden training them up a trellis produces much higher yields per square foot.

Squash blossoms (zucchini is shown here) are prized gourmet food items. Pick only the male blossoms, which tend to be located away from the central stalk and have long, skinny stems with no swelling at their base. Only female stalks turn into squash. But don't harvest all the male blossoms or the female blossoms may not get pollinated.

the garden (bought or homegrown) give you that first cucumber a week or two sooner than seed directly sown into the garden.

How to Plant & Maintain

Cucumbers and summer squash require well-drained, deep soil amended with lots of organic matter. Direct sow seeds into the garden or start with transplants. Thin and space according to seed packet's instructions; five to six plants are usually plenty for a family. Give them plenty of space for sunlight and air circulation.

Add slow-release fertilizer to the soil before planting. Use a balanced fertilizer when planting and again when flowering starts. In midsummer, once the weather is hot, add an organic topdressing, then mulch with compost. This helps keep the soil moist and well fed, which is necessary for top yield and best taste.

Water regularly, especially during dry periods. These tropical plants need a lot of moisture. Avoid watering the leaves as this can promote powdery mildew.

The first flowers are typically male and won't set fruit. Don't worry; the female flowers appear about a week or so later. Female flowers have swollen bases behind the flower and a three-part style inside the flower. One you've seen both, the differences are obvious. After pollination, this becomes the fruit. Without pollinators, cucumbers and squashes will not produce fruit.

To help bees and butterflies find them, interplant with annual flowers. Marigolds and nasturtiums attract pollinators and repel insect pests. These colorful annuals also are reported to improve the taste of cucumber and squash fruits. As an added bonus, marigold and nasturtium flowers are edible just like squash flowers.

There are lots of recipes for squash flowers. Use the male flowers instead of the female flowers so the plant can grow fruit. Place developing fruits on blocks of wood or burlap pieces to keep them clean. Of course, plants grown vertically on a trellis will have cleaner fruit too. But you may need to support them with string to keep large fruit from falling.

Harvesting

Harvesting often *increases* yield. Pickling cucumbers are cut when they are 3 inches long. Slicing cucumbers are best at 6 inches. Large yellowing cucumbers, squashes, and zucchinis are tough and inedible. Although large zucchinis are still edible, they'll have the best flavor when they're smaller. Keep plants picked clean. At the height of the season, you may need to harvest every two days.

Eating

Cucumbers flavor and moisten salads and sandwiches. They have a higher nutritional content if they're left unpeeled. Pickled cucumbers are not nearly as healthy, but they're a tasty treat whole or in relishes.

Unlike pickles, squashes were not childhood favorites. Now I enjoy them all summer steamed, stir-fried, or roasted. My favorite way to eat zucchini is baked with mackerel. Slice the zucchini into finger-sized pieces, place in a cast-iron skillet, and bake at 350 degrees F for 20 minutes. Reduce the heat to 250 degrees F and add smoked mackerel on top. Cook for 10 more minutes while you cut a fresh salad from your garden. Now, *that's* good eating.

FIELD GREENS

LETTUCE
(Aster family)

ARUGULA & MUSTARDS
(Mustard family)

* **Culture:** deep, rich soil; rake soil smooth and level before sowing seed; medium moisture
* **Yield:** ½ to 1 pound per square foot
* **Mature Plant Size:** 12 inches tall x 12 inches wide
* **Where:** raised beds, containers, window boxes, vertical walls, and hanging baskets
* **Ripens:** 8 weeks after planting

Field greens are one of the first crops of the season. And in fall we get another crop. Their lush, decorative foliage in spring hints at the promise of the coming year. Field green seed mixes usually contain a blend of several colorful lettuces, spicy mustards, and savory arugula. Besides being ornamental and tasty, field greens provide nutrition early in the year with vitamins, minerals, and fiber.

 Field greens will grow almost anywhere. Use window boxes, strawberry pots, and wall gardens to maximize space. They are the perfect time-saver crop as you can harvest whenever you like.

Selecting Plants

After sampling, you will know which field greens you like or don't like so much. If something really grabs you, then you can get that specific seed. For me, arugula was the one. Now I grow field greens plus a pack of arugula, just so I'll have enough. Mustards are another of my flavorful favorites. Mizuna has a highly dissected leaf with a sharp, spicy taste. Purple leaf mustard has beautiful foliage and tastes mildly hot.

How to Plant & Maintain

Field greens are perhaps the easiest veggie to grow. They literally grow in fields, so they don't need much. If you prepare the soil well and have a

normal wet spring, then all you do is sow the seeds. Follow the instructions on the packet for spacing and thinning. All thinnings can go directly to the salad bowl. To make sure I use them all, I time thinning the bed to coincide with my desire for a salad.

When the weather gets warm, field greens start to bolt, meaning they begin to sprout a flower stalk and cease new leaf production. The old leaves become bitter and their value as a salad decreases rapidly. By the time they flower, all the leaves will be too tough and bitter to eat. The flowers, though, are fragrant, decorative, and edible. Use them as garnish or in a spring flower arrangement with daffodils and alliums.

Unless you want to collect seed, it's best to dig up and compost field greens during or soon after flowering. If not, you will have field greens volunteering throughout the garden all season. That's not necessarily the worst thing, but it's maybe not what you want.

In late summer, when the peak of the heat has passed, you can sow field greens again for a fall crop. This is a good time to try intercropping. Since field greens will grow in partial shade, they can be sown *beneath* peppers, okra, and beans. When the taller crops are harvested, you'll still have the field greens to harvest until a hard frost (28 degrees F).

Harvesting

Field greens do not form heads, so you can harvest leaves anytime. Unless you are removing the whole plant, do not cut all the leaves. Take the older, outer leaves and allow the younger ones to develop. If you take the younger leaves first, the older leaves will become bitter.

With the arrival of hot weather, field greens can bolt quickly. When you see them start to bolt, you can cut the entire plant and keep it in a sealed container in the refrigerator for a week. Brush off any soil, debris, or insects. Remove any damaged or faded leaves. Do not wash the greens until you are about to eat them.

Eating

Compared to other field greens, lettuces are bland, watery, and sometimes bitter. Even the most succulent lettuce varieties lack the flavor found in mustards. Lettuces are definitely worth growing for fiber and salad filler, but once you've had a burger with arugula or mizuna, you'll never go back to iceberg.

Field greens are most nutritious in a salad. Spring salads with fresh field greens, canned salmon, and an orange bell pepper tastes great. The mustards have a little more versatility than the others. Their stems and leaves are a little tougher, which makes them a nice addition to stir-fry dishes. Add them at the end when there is only about two minutes of cooking time left to add spice *and* crunch.

OKRA
(Mallow family)

* **Culture:** deep, rich soil; medium moisture (especially during flowering); sow as soon as the soil warms to 75°F
* **Yield:** 12 to 20 pods per plants, about 2 pounds per plant
* **Mature Plant Size:** 3 to 10 feet tall x 4 to 6 feet wide
* **Where:** raised beds, large containers, and ornamental gardens
* **Ripens:** 12 to 14 weeks from planting

Okra was my favorite fried vegetable as a kid, even beating out French fries. Now it's my favorite veggie to grow. The queen of ornamental edibles, okra is productive plant with beautiful flowers. It is closely related to flowering hibiscus as its big, bright blossoms attest. They only open early in the morning for one day. By noon, most have been pollinated and are beginning to form pods. But if you miss it one day, don't worry. The plants bloom all summer long. They are a great plant for raised beds.

 Plant dwarf varieties like 'Jade' and 'Lee' and use the standard size varieties as a backdrop in veggie or ornamental gardens. 'Burgundy' and 'Emerald Green Velvet' pods stay tender longer, so you don't have to harvest as often.

Selecting Plants

There are a wide variety of pod colors, sizes, and shapes, but I have not found much difference in taste. 'Burgundy' is truly burgundy colored all over and is one of the most beautiful plants you'll ever grow. 'Burgundy' does not produce the highest yields, but it has less mucilage than most types. For northern gardeners, 'Emerald Green Velvet' and 'White Velvet' will produce into the cooler autumn days better than others.

How to Plant & Maintain

Okra needs open space that is free of all weeds or any other plant competition. Do not sow okra where other crops or plants will shade the seedlings. They need as much sunlight and air circulation as possible.

Okra seeds will *not* germinate until the soil is warm. Sow in late spring or early summer. Soak seeds for a couple hours before planting to speed germination. Space and thin according to the seed packet instructions. Okra plants grow big and tall, so even at a 3-foot spacing, the lower branches will grow together. Twelve well-spaced plants will keep a family in okra through late summer and into autumn.

As a tropical plant, okra is heat loving and it's also drought tolerant. But to increase yield and keep pods tender, water consistently when plants begin to flower. Wait until hot weather to mulch the plants with compost; if soils are too cool, okra will not produce heavily.

Harvesting

Harvest okra often to keep it producing. Otherwise, plants will put energy into ripening a few pods, which become inedible after about a week on the plant. Even if a pod has grown too big and tough to eat, cut it off to spur production of new pods. At peak production okra needs to be harvested nearly every other day.

Eating

Chefs use the mucilage in okra as a natural thickener in gumbos and soups. Eaten raw, okra makes a crisp and juicy component to salads. Frying and roasting remove the slime.

Unfortunately, frying also reduces the natural okra flavor, so now I roast a pan of okra as part of my favorite meal since childhood. Crunchy, roasted okra served with roasted chicken, candied sweet potatoes, and cornbread is a phenomenally good southern dish. Having homegrown veggies to make this meal is one of the main reasons I garden.

ONION

(Onion family)

* **Culture:** deep, rich soil; medium moisture; sow as soon as soil can be worked
* **Yield:** one onion averages 8 ounces, or about 1 to 2 pounds per square foot
* **Mature Plant Size:** 18 inches tall
* **Where:** raised beds, containers, and window boxes
* **Ripens:** 6 to 8 months from seeds, 4 months from sets

Wild onions have been gathered since prehistory for their flavors and medicinal qualities. Ancient cultures like the Egyptians farmed and revered garden onions. Unlike many crops, the bulbs are versatile, easy to store, and easy to transport. It's no surprise the garden onion soon spread throughout the world. Onions are a good crop for small spaces.

 Sow them close together, and use the thinnings in salads. Plant onions with carrots and field greens (called interplanting) to maximize space.

Selecting Plants

Onions are available as seeds or sets (small onion bulbs). As always, many more varieties are available as seed. Onion seed does not store well, so the seed packet should be marked with the current year's packed-for date. Sets should be firm and free of disease or rot; reject soft, brittle, or moldy bulbs.

How to Plant & Maintain

Seeds should take about three weeks to germinate. Sow in rows or blocks in early spring and keep them well watered. Thin to 1 inch apart after they sprout. In a couple weeks, thin again to a 3-inch spacing for smaller bulbs, or an 8-inch spacing for larger bulbs. Thinnings can be eaten as spring onions.

Place sets two-thirds into the ground and water deeply. Space them at 1 inch apart for an early harvest of spring onions. After a couple of weeks, thin as with seeds according to the desired bulb size.

Onions need regular watering during hot, dry weather to keep actively growing and enlarging their bulbs. Remove and discard any bulbs that show disease or begin to flower.

In areas with mild winters, a fall crop can be planted. Although onions are hardy perennials, in cold climates large bulbs are prone to split.

Harvesting

Onions will "show" you when they are ready to harvest. When the bulbs look swollen and about three-fourths of the leaves have fallen over, the onions are ready. *Carefully* dig them up. Cut the roots off 1 inch below the bulb. Cut the neck 2 inches above the bulb.

Keep the outer skin (tunic) intact while harvesting. The tunic protects the bulb's flesh from damage, disease, and desiccation. Let bulbs dry for an hour or so outside. Gently brush any excess soil from the bulb. Place the bulbs a warm, dry area indoors to further dry for a couple of days. Again, remove any remaining dirt or debris. Store in a cool, dark, dry place.

Eating

Until I began growing onions, I never realized how versatile and universal they were. Eaten raw, they add zest to salads and sandwiches. Cook small onions with meat dishes. In recipes, onions enhance nearly every meat or vegetable dish. Roasting, baking, and stir-frying make them noticeably sweeter.

PEAS
(Bean family)

* **Culture:** deep, rich soil; medium moisture; provide vertical support, harvest often
* **Yield:** ½ pound per planting, ½ to 2 pounds per square foot
* **Mature Plant Size:** 1 to 6 feet tall x 2 feet wide
* **Where:** large containers, trellises, fences, railings, poles
* **Ripens:** 8 weeks for sugar and snow peas; 10 weeks for English peas

Freshly picked garden peas are often the first fruiting veggie of the season. Sometimes peas don't even make it to the kitchen because they make a quick, tasty, nutritious snack in the garden. If you can hold out, have the table set and water boiling before you go to the garden to pick them. Peas have two good traits for small spaces: they grow vertically and can be harvested early. They will neatly grow up a trellis, and be done in time to plant cucumbers or beans.

 Look for dwarf varieties, like 'Little Marvel' and 'Meteor', which will grow in hanging baskets. For regular varieties use vertical supports to maximize space.

Selecting Plants

There are several types and varieties of peas. Plant early and late types together to extend the season, or make successive plantings of one variety from week to week. Smooth, round peas are more cold tolerant but less sweet than ones with wrinkled skin. Snow peas, sugar peas, and others have tender, edible pods. They are typically used in stir-fry dishes.

How to Plant & Maintain

Peas are cool-weather crops, but they can't take frosty temperatures. Pea seeds will rot in cold, soggy conditions. Sow them once the soil begins to warm in spring. Peas sometimes germinate sporadically, so sow thickly or plant a few extra in pots to fill in any gaps in the row later. Space and thin according to the seed packet instructions.

Peas are deep rooted and drought tolerant. They really only need regular watering as they sprout and when they begin to flower. Consistent watering when they flower increases the number of pea pods.

Peas are vines and need support to grow, but any trellis or staking system will do. Or make your own supports. Put 5-foot-tall posts or sticks down the pea rows every 2 feet. Attach sturdy string or wire across the posts at every 12 inches of height to make a gridlike support system for the vines.

If your growing season is not too short, you can also plant a fall crop of peas. Count back 12 weeks from the first frost date for fall, and sow then. This gives the peas enough time to ripen before a killing frost.

Harvesting

Harvest sugar and snow pea pods as soon as the pods stop lengthening. Harvest English peas when the pods stop lengthening and the seeds are swollen inside. Like most fruiting veggies, you have to harvest regularly to keep the plant in production.

Sugar compounds in peas begin to break down rapidly after picking, so plan to eat them within hours of picking to get the best flavor. Knowing this will help you avoid embarrassing situations. A few years ago I was bragging to my mom and sister about our tasty, super sweet peas. I told them they were the best ever and I'd bring them some. After the 12-hour drive and six hours of sleep, my spectacular peas were like cardboard. The lesson: pick 'em right before you eat 'em. Blanched or cooked peas will keep their flavor much longer.

Eating

Peapods are delicious raw in salads or stir-fried with other vegetables. A classic preparation is to boil them for a few minutes in a little water with fresh-ground black pepper, salt, and rosemary, and then serve them with mashed potatoes and baked rainbow trout.

English or snap peas develop big, sweet peas. You may have to remove the fibrous string before eating the pods though. Shelling peas have tough inedible pods that are loaded with succulent peas.

PEPPERS, SWEET & CHILI

(Nightshade family)

* **Culture:** rich, fertile soil; medium moisture; provide support when fruits form
* **Yield:** depends on the variety, generally 5 to 30 peppers or about
    2 to 5 pounds per plant
* **Mature Plant Size:** 2 to 4 feet tall x 2 to 4 feet wide
* **Where:** raised beds, containers, window boxes, and hanging baskets
* **Ripens:** 6 to 8 weeks after transplanting for chili peppers and green peppers;
    10 to 12 weeks for colorful sweet peppers

Sweet peppers decorate the garden and the plate. They are tasty, nutritious, ornamental, and economical. Organic sweet peppers are often the most expensive veggies in the market. Because I like organic sweet peppers and I don't have Bill Gates' money, sweet peppers are indispensible in my veggie garden. I look at a productive sweet pepper plant like a money bush.

Chili peppers are addictive. Once you start eating them, you want more. Fortunately, they are easy to grow. Gardeners can satisfy their craving for heat with only a few plants. Unless you are hosting a chili cook-off, five chili pepper plants will give you more than enough chilies for your family and heat-loving friends.

 Interplant with carrots to maximize space. Harvest sweet peppers when green to maximize production. Or wait until sweet peppers turn colors for the sweetest fruits.

Selecting Plants

Peppers are available as seeds and transplants. Growing from seed is simple and the least expensive way to grow peppers. Many heirlooms and hybrids are offered *only* as seed. Unlike tomatoes, though, there is little taste difference between pepper heirlooms and hybrids. While it's always exciting to grow an heirloom, beginners may want to start with hybrids for their extra disease resistance.

Sweet peppers as used here are less than 2,500 units on the Scoville scale, a measurement of chili pepper heat. Some sweet peppers have no heat, including 'Bell' (0), 'Gypsy' (0), 'Banana Supreme' (0), 'Carmen' (0). Other sweet peppers, like pimiento (pimento) (200) and ancho (2500), are mildly spicy. Chili peppers bring on the heat and sizzle. They are on the high end of the heat scale with jalapeños (8,000), cayennes (30,000), habañeros (300,000), and finally the 'Naga Jolokia' ghost chili (1,000,000!). If you are new to hot chilies, start with 'Hungarian Hot Wax' and 'Jalapeño' before you move to the big boys.

Planting your pepper plant in a shroud made from plastic pipe helps keep the root system warm and safe—which peppers *love*.

How to Plant & Maintain

Before planting, prepare the soil with amendments to improve fertility and drainage. Space plants 18 to 24 inches apart in rows or blocks. Water the transplants regularly as they are establishing. Once plants begin to set fruit, stake or cage them. Heavy fruit can drag the branches down or even break them. At the arrival of hot weather (usually around the same time they need staking), mulch pepper plants with compost or leaf mold to conserve water and build the soil.

Peppers are the perfect veggie for container gardening; use 16-inch pots to give them best chance for success. Container peppers require more fertilizing than in-ground peppers. Every two weeks feed them with foliar fertilizer at one-fourth strength. Add an organic topdressing or other slow-release fertilizer to the pot in late spring and again in midsummer. Peppers don't require a lot of fertilizer to live, but they produce more fruits when adequately fertilized.

Active pollinators also increase fruit production. Combine peppers with low-growing herbs and flowers, such as oregano, lemon thyme, and alyssum. The open branching structure of pepper plants allows light to reach ground-level plants. Oregano and alyssum bloom all growing season and will attract pollinators to the pepper flowers.

Harvesting

Sweet peppers are edible as soon as they form, but many green peppers are somewhat bitter. If you allow them to fully ripen, sweet peppers actually taste sweet. But to fully ripen a sweet pepper can take an additional two to four weeks after the fruit has reached full size. Although they're not completely ripe, green peppers are still nutritious and better tasting than most from your neighborhood store.

And that causes a conundrum that I face every year: quantity versus quality. Harvesting peppers promotes more peppers. Not harvesting peppers causes production to cease. You can get a lot more immature, green, not-as-sweet peppers than you can fully ripened, colorful sweet peppers. The last couple of years my solution has been simple: grow more pepper plants! With at least two plants of each type, I can let one plant ripen a few fruits to maturity and harvest loads of green peppers

from the other.

Fully ripe fruits can't remain on the plant indefinitely without losing quality. Harvest peppers when they turn their ultimate color and are still plump and firm. If the pepper skin starts to wrinkle, decay is beginning, so harvest and use immediately. Cut the pepper with some stalk still attached.

Chili peppers are certainly edible when they're not ripe, but they have a lower nutritional content and will not store. Ripe chili peppers are perfect for drying. Because gardeners throughout time have harvested more chili peppers than they could use, there are several methods for drying.

The easiest way to dry chilies is to pull or cut the entire plant before frost. Hang the plant in a dry, frost-free area until the skins are leathery. Another option is to tie individual peppers on a string and make a colorful ristra. Ristras are those decorative garlands of peppers that you often see hanging in restaurants. Once their skin becomes leathery, store chilies in a jar or plastic bag in a cool, dark, dry place. If they are left hanging out, chilies can gather dust and lose their color.

Eating

Sweet peppers are fantastic roasted, grilled, or sautéed. But a garden fresh pepper is best raw in salads. The bright color, sweet taste, and crisp texture change a common salad into a masterpiece. The audible crunch screams freshness in every bite. It's hard not to be smugly happy when you are enjoying a late summer garden salad of your tomatoes, spinach, arugula, beans, and oregano topped with brightly colored sweet peppers.

For those who like it hot, chili peppers enhance every dish. Chilies add *zing* to sauces, soups, and (of course) chili. I like them more each year. Invite your friends over for the game and serve thick, medium to medium-well grilled burgers topped with Swiss cheese and chili peppers accompanied by tall glasses of ale to put out the fire.

POTATOES

(Nightshade family)

* **Culture:** deep, loose, rich soil; medium moisture; cover the bases of stems with straw as they grow taller
* **Yield:** 1 to 3 pounds per plant
* **Mature Plant Size:** 2 to 3 feet tall x 2 to 3 feet wide
* **Where:** raised beds and large containers
* **Ripens:** 12 to 16 weeks after transplanting outside

Potatoes are one of the most popular veggies in the world. Even kids love potatoes, which is a good reason to let children grow them. They are an easy way to introduce kids to gardening. Plus, potatoes come in a wide range of fun colors and shapes. Growing blue fingerling potatoes is a fabulously fun and tasty project for a kid.

Choose tall containers to increase production of potato tubers.
Interplant with bush beans to maximize space and increase soil fertility.

Selecting Plants

The types of potato are early, midseason, and late. Early and midseason potatoes do not store well and should be eaten fresh. Late potatoes are typically stored for winter use. All types can be planted in spring as soon as soils begin to warm. The planting season extends to early summer for midseason and late types. This lends potatoes to successive plantings to extend the harvest season over several months.

There are hundreds of potato varieties within the different types. Many heirlooms were specifically developed for certain regions. Check with your local Extension Service or botanic garden to learn about varieties suited for your area. Potatoes are susceptible to a lot of diseases in the commercial fields, but these diseases are rarely a problem for home gardens. Just to be safe, buy from sources with certified disease-free sets.

How to Plant & Maintain

Before planting, prepare the soil with amendments to improve fertility, texture, and drainage. Potatoes require a deep, loose soil for large smooth taters. If you don't have sandy soil, incorporate some sand in your garden soil along with compost, potash, and slow-release fertilizer. Use a low-nitrogen fertilizer (1-2-2 or 5-10-10, for example) at planting and again in early summer. Add organic topdressing or a slow-release fertilizer before planting and in midsummer.

Mulch plants one week after they sprout and keep a thick layer of mulch on them throughout the season. The mulch layer keeps the soil cooler, which helps tuber development (tubers stop forming when soil reaches 80 degrees F). Mulch also keeps developing potatoes in

Gently scrape away soil around the base of the potato plant to gauge the size and growth progress of the potatoes. Replace the soil.

the dark; if sunlight hits the potatoes, they will turn green and become inedible. Add soil or straw every week to keep developing tubers covered. Straw is the better choice because it makes harvesting easier. The mulch layer should keep weeds at bay. If you have to weed, work carefully so you don't damage the tubers

Potatoes are drought tolerant, but consistent watering increases yields. Water regularly during their active growth, but do not allow them to become waterlogged.

Potatoes grow well in deep containers, especially if you use the straw method. Put 6 inches of compost on the bottom and lay the sets on top. Cover with a couple inches of straw, then water. As the plants grow, continue to add straw. Occasionally add a layer of grass clippings or dark compost to make sure sunlight cannot reach the developing tubers. This method makes harvesting easy and gives you clean potatoes.

Harvesting

Potatoes, especially early and midseason varieties, can be harvested through-out summer and autumn. Check their size before harvesting by gently scraping back the soil to expose some tubers. If the tubers are full sized, use a garden fork to lift the entire plant out of the ground.

Late potatoes can be left in the ground until the tops die back. Let the skins harden for a week or two in ground. Then, gently lift them. Let potatoes dry in the sun for a few hours. Once they're dry, brush off the dirt without damaging the skin. Store undamaged potatoes in a cool, dark, dry place.

Eating

Everyone loves potatoes. Roasted potatoes with grilled fish and fresh veggies always make a supremely satisfying meal. Lately, my favorite potato recipe is adapted from the television show *America's Test Kitchen*. Cut a potato into quarter-inch-thick slices. Boil for 15 minutes and drain. Add salt and olive oil; stir with a wooden spoon or spatula. Place the slices flat on a large pan or cast-iron skillet and roast in a 350 degree F convection oven (preferably). Cook until crispy, turning once or twice. These crunchy taters are delectable with breakfast, lunch, or dinner.

SWEET POTATOES

(Morning Glory family)

* **Culture:** deep, loose, rich soil; medium moisture, especially during the hottest part of summer
* **Yield:** depends on the climate, generally 4 to 8 sweet potatoes or about 3 to 5 pounds per plant
* **Mature Plant Size:** 6 feet or more spreading groundcover, vines root as they sprawl across the ground
* **Where:** raised beds and large, deep containers
* **Ripens:** 15 to 18 weeks after transplanting outside

Heat-loving sweet potatoes may be my favorite vegetable. They are a super food loaded with Vitamin A, Vitamin C, Vitamin E, dietary fiber, antioxidants, and more. I didn't know about their health benefits until I began gardening. Sweet potatoes are a childhood favorite of mine because they taste so *good*! Growing up in South Carolina, we had them a couple of times a week. That sweet, creamy, rich flavor had me hooked before I could talk.

 In cold climates start sweet potatoes indoors to get a jump on the growing season. Do not plant outside until the soil is warm. Train or tie vines to a trellis or fence to use your vertical space.

Selecting Plants

Sweet potato slips should be healthy, flexible, and undamaged. Reject those that are dry and brittle. Garden centers probably won't have much selection, but lots of types are available online and at seed-and-feed stores in the country. Gardeners in northern climates should choose early maturing varieties.

The easiest way to get sweet potato slips is to grow your own from a batch you liked. Sweet potatoes that sprout in the cupboard make it easy. Just break off the sprouts and place in small pot of moist soil mix. The vines will lengthen and become slips. Once a root system and true leaves appear, they are ready for the garden. Or you can pot them up in separate containers and treat them like houseplants until warm weather arrives. Starting slips as houseplants is a good trick for short season gardeners. It lets you begin with more established plants, which yield more sweet potatoes.

In all my years of growing sweet potatoes, I have grown the same plant. My great-grandmother, Mrs. Ruth, gave me a slip in 1998. That first year had a small harvest, but I saved the tiny sweet potato and vine pieces. After overwintering them as houseplants, they were ready to go when warm weather arrived. Now I keep one sweet potato plant as a cherished houseplant, so I can cut slips anytime for the garden or to share.

How to Plant & Maintain

Before planting, prepare the soil with amendments to improve fertility, texture, and drainage. Sweet potatoes require a deep, loose soil for large smooth taters. If you don't have sandy soil, incorporate some sand in your garden soil along with compost, potash, and slow-release fertilizer. Use a low-nitrogen fertilizer (1-2-2 or 5-10-10, for example) when planting and again in midsummer. Add organic topdressing or a slow-release fertilizer in midsummer.

As you wait for warm weather you can start your own sweet potato "slips." Root sprouts from a sweet potato in water until a good root system forms, and then transplant them into containers until you can plant them outside.

Don't think about planting sweet potatoes until warm weather arrives. The hotter it is, the better they'll grow. Mound soil into hills or raised rows. When planting slips, remove all lower leaves so that only two or three sets remain near the tip. Place the slip two-thirds into the ground. Space hills or rows 3 feet apart and individual slips 6 to 12 inches apart.

Edible sweet potatoes grow in containers just like ornamental sweet potatoes. Choose a well-drained soil mix and a big pot. A 20-inch pot will hold three slips. Amend the soil mix with compost and potash, but you don't need sand in a container; the soil mix is loose enough.

Sweet potatoes are drought tolerant, but consistent moisture will increase yields. Water regularly the first two weeks after transplanting and again during weeks 8 through 12. Those are the critical times of root establishment and tuberous root production. Consistent watering at the right time produces the best results.

Harvesting

Temperatures below 40 degrees F can damage vines and the tubers. Harvest well before the first frost. Stop watering two weeks before harvesting. Cut vines back to the ground one week before harvesting. This will help toughen a sweet potato's fragile skin.

Carefully dig them up. The garden fork lifts taters without as much damage. I've cut through too many to ever use a shovel again. Dig a little wider and deeper than you expect. Sweet potatoes have a way of rambling. Collect the small tubers with attached stems to grow indoors for next year's slip production. Prune the roots and stems off large ones.

Spread uncleaned sweet potatoes out to dry for a couple hours. Bring them indoors and continue to let them dry for another day. Then, gently clean off excess dirt with a soft bristle brush or rag. After they are clean, begin the curing process to increase the sugar content. Place the harvest in a warm (85 degrees F) and humid (90 percent) spot for a week. You don't have to be as exact as professional growers. I put my taters in a clear plastic storage box and place the box in the warmest area of the house. After they've cured, store sweet potatoes in dark, dry, cool place. Properly dried and cured, they last up to 10 months.

To harvest container-grown sweet potatoes, simply invert and empty the container. The potatoes tend to grow on the very bottom.

Eating

When I started gardening in Chicago, I was a complete novice and did not know sweet potatoes were a southern crop. All I knew was that you should grow what you like to eat and I liked to eat sweet potatoes. My first crop was small, but since then, I have made several adjustments to successfully grow this tropical vine in a northern clime. Fortunately, sweet potatoes grow well in large containers and raised beds.

Sweet potatoes are prominent in Thai curries and Japanese maki, but once again Southerners do it best. Roasted chicken, roasted okra, and cornbread with candied sweet potatoes is my all-time favorite meal. After a couple helpings, all you can do is lie back, watch football, and promise you'll work off the calories next week.

There are lots of variations on the recipe, but my sister Rochelle showed me the fastest way to candy sweet potatoes. Cut three to four medium sweet potatoes into eight quarter-inch slices. Get out your largest frying pan, like a chicken fryer. Turn the burner to low to medium low. Add one-half stick of butter, melted, or 4 tablespoons of olive oil to the fryer. Lay the sliced sweet potatoes in the pan. You can stack them two layers high. Add ½ cup of sugar or more, to your taste. Sprinkle at least 1 teaspoon of nutmeg and 1 teaspoon of vanilla on top. While you start the cornbread, check back every five minutes to swirl the pan. This keeps anything from sticking. As the cornbread is coming out of the oven or about 30 minutes later, the sweet potatoes will be tender and flavorful.

A cold frame, shown here, is a great place to start sweet potato vines until the weather warms enough to plant out in the garden.

TOMATOES

(Nightshade family)

* **Culture:** fertile soil; above average moisture; provide support
   while plants are still small
* **Yield:** 5 to 8 pounds per plant
* **Mature Plant Size:** 3 to 6 feet tall x 2 to 4 feet wide
* **Where:** raised beds, containers, window boxes, and hanging baskets
* **Ripens:** 8 to 12 weeks after transplanting, 16 to 20 weeks from seed

Every neighborhood in the world has someone growing tomatoes. They are the most popular homegrown veggie for good reasons. The plants produce a big harvest. Tomatoes contain lots of vitamins and minerals. Most important, you can grow tomatoes anywhere you have bright sun, 60 warm days, and at least 6 inches of soil.

 For very small spaces and hanging planters, use early-ripening and small fruited varieties. Provide strong supports (modular or wire cages) so plants can grow vertically.

How to Plant & Maintain

Space tomatoes 18 to 24 inches apart in rows or blocks. Stake or cage them once they are 18 inches tall and actively growing. There are lots of options for staking tomatoes. Tomatoes grow rampantly in mid- and late summer. Select a cage that's big enough to hold the tomato all season. If you don't want to start with a big cage right away, modular cages can be adjusted as the tomato grows.

In midsummer, mulch tomato plants with compost or leaf mold to suppress weeds, build the soil, and conserve moisture. Tomatoes are drought tolerant and do not need regular watering to survive. But following a watering schedule that keeps the soil moist (not wet) improves production and limits skin cracking.

Tomatoes grow well in containers. Large pots, 16 inches diameter or greater, give them the best chance for success. But even hanging pots can produce a big crop of tomatoes. When grown in containers, feed every two weeks with one-fourth-strength foliar fertilizer. Add organic topdressing or a slow-release fertilizer in late spring and midsummer.

Harvesting

Tomatoes come off the vines into your hand when they're ripe. A gentle tug is all that's needed. Check your plants regularly to avoid missing any. Many tomatoes will become overripe and rotten if left on the plant too long, so search all through the foliage.

At the end of the season, before frost, many indeterminate tomatoes are still loaded with unripe fruits. Most of them will ripen, although the flavor is diminished compared to vine-ripened ones from summer. The other option is to use them green.

My cousin George always brings in baskets of green tomatoes before frost. He uses some for fried green tomatoes but most of them are prepared into many jars of chow-chow relish. George readily shares this southern treat with friends and families. I look forward to getting mine every Christmas. It's a great way to keep the taste of summer on hand.

Eating

From salads to sauces, tomatoes work with any meal. Few things can rival a flavorful 'Cherokee Purple' tomato sliced on a plate with seasoned salt. But I found one—roasting tomatoes in a cast-iron skillet. The roasting concentrates the flavor and brings out a natural sweetness. Use roasted tomatoes on pasta or in rice dishes.

To roast tomatoes, dice them and add to a cast-iron skillet with olive oil. Season with salt and pepper. Cover with a lid or foil so they don't dry out. Put them in a preheated oven on 350 degrees F for 30 minutes. Check to see if they have reduced enough. If so, taste. Add fresh herbs from the garden and serve.

Chapter 5

GET OUT & GROW! TOMATOES

TOMATOES ARE THE MOST COMMON homegrown veggie worldwide. Their popularity is linked to how easily they grow and big yields. Few other small space garden plants can grow as many fruits in one season. Tomatoes also contain many healthy vitamins and antioxidants. However, nutrition, low maintenance, and high productivity are all secondary to taste. People grow tomatoes because they are delicious.

Tomato flavors range from sweet to acrid, meaty to juicy, and complex to mild. There's a variety for every palate. Many are delicious fresh, and cooking seems to intensify the flavor. Nearly every culture has found a way to incorporate tomatoes into their favorites dishes. Where would modern cuisine be without tomato sauces? Could we survive in a world without ketchup, salsa, and lasagna? People have thought of numerous ways to preserve tomatoes. When you have a glut of fruit with a short shelf life, you've got to figure out something. Saucing, canning, freezing, or drying them allows you to cook with tomatoes year-round. My great-grandmother, Mrs. Ruth, would can dozens of mason jars filled with tomatoes and chow-chow salsa in late summer. (That generation was always worried about the next Great Depression.) Since the winters invariably passed without incidents of food rationing, in spring she would give jars of the previous summer's goodness to family and neighbors.

But I have a confession. Even though I grew up in South Carolina with a farming grandfather and canning great-grandmother, I never liked tomatoes. Maybe the varieties my family grew were too acidic for my young taste buds. Actually, I can't remember eating them fresh. They were always canned or sauced. By my teen years, I thought all raw tomatoes tasted like that bland, watery, mealy, pale thing that was sliced onto my fast-food hamburger, which I immediately picked off my sandwich and tossed in the garbage.

Now I've seen the light! The "ah-ha" moment came in my second season when I grew 'Garden Peach' and 'Brandywine'. 'Garden Peach' was the first tomato I tasted fresh that I actually liked. It was flavorful, it wasn't mealy, and it wasn't too acidic. I finally knew what all the fuss was about. Since then, we make space for tomatoes every year.

Once you have had a good homegrown tomato, you're hooked. It is easy to see why they were cultivated throughout South and Central America for thousands of years. Their rapid spread to the rest of the world is just as logical. In a span of a couple hundred years, tomatoes convinced mankind to grow and nurture them in every corner of the globe. Their luxuriant growth, easy cultivation, nutrient levels, and savory taste make them perfect for backyard gardeners from Bolivia to Bulgaria, from Morocco to Thailand, and from New Zealand to New York. You are just as likely to find tomatoes in a courtyard in Italy as in a balcony container in Detroit.

The Tomato Story

Despite being cultivated for hundreds of years throughout the world, tomatoes still defy classification by scientists. *Lycopersicon lycopersicon*, *Lycopersicon esculenta*, and *Solanum lycopersicon* all are acceptable scientific names for the same plant. Scientists thought tomatoes were in their own specific category (*Lycopersicon*), but new genetic research has shown them to be just another type of nightshade (*Solanum*), like potato and eggplant. So if you are ordering from a catalog or online, don't be confused by the varying scientific names.

The word *Lycopersicon* means "wolf apple" and comes from the seventeenth-century western European belief that tomatoes were dangerous and deceptive. Strangely, tomatoes were considered poisonous despite the fact that the Spanish had been eating them since importing the crop from Mexico in the sixteenth century.

Garden tomatoes originate from a South American perennial vine. That plant was cultivated thousands of years ago in the Andes. The Spanish introduced the tomato to Europe and their colonies throughout the world. It was a welcomed source of Vitamin C on long sailing voyages. Italians, Eastern Europeans, Filipinos, and Eastern Asians all quickly adopted the tomato as a staple crop. England and its colonies were slow to use tomatoes for anything except ornamental plantings. But soon the whole world knew that the beautiful tomato fruits were tasty, not toxic. By the early 1900s, tomatoes were accepted as the ultimate homegrown fruit.

Technically a Fruit, Legally a Vegetable

With seeds surrounded by flesh, tomatoes are the textbook definition of a fruit. Botanically, they are a berry. However, people call them veggies and plant them in veggie gardens. There are two reasons for this: culinary and legal. Apples, grapes, blackberries, and other fruits are usually really sweet. Since most tomatoes are more savory than sweet, people naturally group them with veggies.

Legally, tomatoes were classified as vegetables for tax purposes by the Supreme Court in 1893. Since vegetables were taxed and fruits were not, the Nix brothers, who were grocers, sued Edward Hedden, the tax collector of the Port of New York, to get back duties they paid on tomatoes. The court chose the trade definition over the scientific one and ruled in favor of the defendant. The ruling stated that vegetables were classified by use and since tomatoes were served at dinner, not as dessert, they were commonly thought of as vegetables. This court made it clear that this was a legal classification based solely within the context of the Tariff Act of 1883 and did not apply botanically or scientifically. Not even tomatoes can escape politics.

Perfect Small Space Veggie

Tomatoes adapt to different growing conditions. Like most garden veggies, they would prefer to grow in a sunny, sheltered, well-manicured garden with deep, rich soil. But they don't require that. By nature tomatoes are drought-tolerant, pest-resistant ramblers. They're tough. If we can supply the basics (sun, soil, water, fertilizer), they usually take care of the rest.

Tomatoes are one of the best veggies for small space gardeners because of their tenacity and ability to grow in tight spaces. With their scrambling habit, they can grow among and over other plants. Open space is appreciated, but it's fine to plant them within flowerbeds and among informal hedges. When adding them to ornamental gardens, place large varieties toward the back where they won't overwhelm smaller plants.

Tall in the back, short in the front is a basic principle of design that I learned the hard way in the first season growing tomatoes at the community garden. 'Better Boy' tomatoes were planted near the front of the flowerbed, simply because it was within easy reach. After a few weeks, they were flopping over and shading the smaller zinnias and petunias. By the end of the season, my "flowerbed" was actually a tangle of tomatoes. If I had planted correctly, there would have been tomatoes and flowers.

If you want to plant tomatoes in the front or middle of ornamental beds, choose smaller determinant varieties. They won't overwhelm the space and can be supported with small, inconspicuous cages. Plus, because determinants ripen many fruits at once, they'll add a burst of color and unique texture to the flowerbed.

No Yard? No Problem

Tomatoes grow best in the ground, but they produce well in containers too. Do you need a big space or even land to grow good tomatoes? As long as you have an outdoor space with eight hours of light, you can grow tomatoes. Because the community plot with my main crop is a couple miles from home, I always grow some tomatoes in containers on my balcony. Nothing beats stepping out your door to pick a fresh tomato,

whether it's your backyard door or your balcony door.

Despite the deep, extensive root system of in-ground tomatoes, nearly all varieties can adapt to the limited soil volume in containers. In sunny, sheltered locations tomatoes grow well in containers. If your space is windy and exposed, smaller fruited, quick-ripening types (patios and cherries) give you a better chance at a bigger crop. In less than ideal conditions, the longer the fruit takes to ripen, the more likely that circumstances or neglect will reduce your container harvest.

This was another hard lesson learned on my rooftop a few years ago. I planted some 'Brandywine' (late-ripening heirloom variety) tomatoes in huge 24-inch pots. First a May hailstorm stunted them. Then some sloppy contractors spilled a caulking dust that burned many of the leaves. Before they could fully recover, strong bursts of wind from a vicious July storm broke a few of the branches. It wasn't until mid-September that I got the first 'Brandywine' tomato, and I didn't get many. By contrast, the patio, grape, and 'Yellow Pear' varieties suffered the same accidents, but still ripened fruit by mid-August and kept producing.

Because of conditions, urban gardeners are often apprehensive about gardening. I have lived in apartment or condo buildings for the past 20 years, so I understand their frustrations. Without the right materials, plants, and information, container gardening can be challenging. So here you go. First you need a container at least 16 inches in diameter. The bigger the container, the better the tomato grows. More soil equals more roots, which yield more fruits.

Recently I started growing a few tomatoes in an EarthBox®, a self-watering container garden (29 inches long by 14 inches wide by 11 inches high) and in the Regal Vine Planter from Designer Planters, Inc.® (28 inches in diameter by 22 inches high). The first season, there were more tomatoes than ever, and I credit the larger containers for that. Know your limits, though. Moving a Regal Vine Planter is no easy task.

Potting soil mix is the most crucial component to growing tasty tomatoes in containers. Potting soil mix is very different from garden soil. These mixes are lightweight, well drained, high in organic matter, sterile (disease and weed free), and typically nutritionally balanced. Depending on where you live, your garden soil may be heavy clay, poorly drained, full of harmful bacteria, weedy, buggy, too acidic, too basic, and/or nutritionally imbalanced. In the ground there is a big enough soil community to moderate many of these issues, but in a container the problems are magnified and may affect yield. *Never* dig soil from the garden for containers. Buy a quality potting soil mix and you will be happier with the results.

The Basics

The basic necessities for growing great tomatoes are eight or more hours of sunlight, ample water, well-drained fertile soil, and a little attention. That's all you need, whether you garden on a 5-acre farm or in a patio container. The only requirement that's tricky is the fertile soil. Amending the planting area with compost and calcium-rich fertilizer before planting is an important step. Good soil makes delectable tomatoes.

If you have 60 days of warm weather (daytime temperatures from 70 degrees F to 85 degrees F), you can successfully grow tomatoes. Even our friends to the north in Alaska can get a crop of 'Glacier' tomatoes during their shortened summer.

Fortunately, in most gardens tomatoes will grow rampant like weeds. I bumbled my way to a decent harvest of 'Early Girl' tomatoes in my first year without knowing anything about soil, plants, or gardening. I used scissors as pruners and watered with a bucket. I don't think I even owned a trowel.

In my second season, good fortune blessed me with a fairy garden mother, Master Gardener Ruth Mesulius. Ruth started me out with heirloom seedlings, sage advice, and encouragement. When you are a newbie, encouragement is often the most important part. You don't need years of experience to grow good tomatoes, just good info with a side of luck.

Of course there were mistakes and mishaps. I did not expect such unchecked growth and was not prepared to support the tomato plants. They flopped *all over* the place. Voles and squirrels at the community garden took bites out of many tomatoes, rendering them useless. Voles—which look like fat, burrowing mice—have a habit of taking a few bites out of a tomato and then moving on to a new one. They never come back to finish what they've started. Pill bugs, earwigs, slugs, and fungi then move in to the damaged tomatoes, making them extra gooey and gross.

Despite all this, my wife, Natasha, and I had a huge harvest of 'Better Boy' and 'Sungold' with plenty of 'Garden Peach' our second year. Natasha loves everything about tomatoes and was thrilled just to touch the leaves. The furry foliage gives off a distinct scent that reminds her of childhood summers spent in her grandparents' garden. So since then, tomatoes have been a staple in our garden.

How to Grow Tomatoes

Soil

My friend Chad, a certified organic farmer who used to play ball with me in ages past, told me that the soil is the *key* to growing delicious tomatoes. Good soil makes a good tomato great. I've tasted the proof firsthand. He has worked mounds of organic amendments into his fields to create a rich, loamy soil well stocked with minerals.

While you are mixing organic matter into your tomato bed, add some calcium too. Calcium is an important nutrient for tomatoes. Without it, fruits get blossom-end rot, which ruins tomatoes. Calcium tends to stay put in the soil. Dig down 4 to 8 inches to the root zone and apply the calcium before planting. Bone meal, gypsum, lime, dolomite, and tomato fertilizers are available at garden centers. Retailers should be able to tell you which products are best for tomatoes.

If you compost, there are many calcium sources in your kitchen scraps. I save my eggshells and clamshells just for my tomato plantings. You have to wash them out thoroughly; you don't want any nasty bacteria or rats to show up. Once washed and dried, they should be coarsely crushed and put aside for mixing into compost or soil in early spring. Eggshells and clamshells are not the only household items comprised mostly of calcium carbonate. Some gardeners amend tomato plantings with powdered milk, expired vitamins, or antacids. Regardless of the source, amending with organic matter and calcium will give you the best start for growing healthy tomatoes.

Sunlight

Tomatoes *love* the sunshine. Eight hours of sun a day provides enough energy for high-yielding plants, but they'll take as much light as they can get. When selecting a spot for tomatoes, pick the sunniest space possible for you to easily tend. Avoid planting too close to trees or buildings that may shade them during the day.

The exception is in extremely hot areas, such as San Antonio or Miami. Tomatoes may stop producing when temperatures reach triple digits during the day and are above 75 degrees F at night. In climates where hot is the norm, plant in partial shade to keep tomatoes cooler and productive for a longer period. Planting in spots with northern or eastern exposure keeps them out of the merciless afternoon sun.

Some small space gardeners have limited sunlight. Urban gardens are often shaded by buildings and trees. If you have less than six hours of sunlight, your garden will struggle to grow full-sized tomatoes.

Try cherry varieties, which can fruit (though not heavily) in partial shade. Or plant some elephant ears in your shady space, then look into getting a sunnier spot for growing veggies at your local community garden.

Watering

Tomatoes like mesic soil moisture, which means keeping the soil moist— not wet. They are drought-tolerant plants by nature, but they need ample moisture to produce a big crop of fruits. Do not allow the soil to dry completely between watering. When the soil dries out, plants can suffer from blossom-end rot, cracked skin, and wilting.

As always, try to water early in the morning—dawn is best. That gives the water a chance to soak into the root zone before the sun's evaporative powers can steal any away. Some gardeners water at night to avoid evaporation, but night watering can promote fungal diseases, such as powdery mildew on tomatoes.

When loaded with fruit and leaves, tomatoes use a lot of water, especially in containers. During August when the hot, dry southwestern winds

A spraying wand delivers the water right to the base of the tomato plant where it is needed. And it causes zero erosion of soil around the plant.

blow across my rooftop garden, my tomatoes have to be watered daily. The largest plants in the biggest planters can require a gallon or more a day. In-ground plantings typically fare much better. Watering twice a week is enough to get them through the heat waves in most soils. However, in sandy, hot areas, even in-ground plants may need daily watering too.

The best way to tell if plants need water is the finger test. Put your finger in the soil up the first knuckle. Pull your finger out. If it is moist, you don't need to water. If it's dry, water right away. Once you have done this a few times, you'll be able to detect visual clues from the plant, such as a loss in vigor or a paler color. Learn to recognize these signs before the leaves begin to droop. Try to avoid any wilting, which can stunt plants and cause fruit drop.

Fertilizing

Tomatoes are heavy feeders. Amend the soil with rich organic matter before planting. When you transplant them to the garden, give them some fertilizer. Choose one high in phosphorus (the middle number) and add a calcium supplement. Or select a specially formulated tomato fertilizer that contains additional calcium. Follow the directions. Do *not* overfertilize. In particular, avoid too much nitrogen, which encourages tomatoes to grow lots of leaves and vines, sometimes at the expense of flowers and fruit.

Mulching

A thick layer of mulch helps keep soil evenly moist and inhibits weeds. It also helps fight diseases by absorbing raindrops, which prevents them from splashing bacteria-laden soil onto the tomato leaves. If you mulch with compost, rotted manure, leaf mold, or other organic mulch, you're feeding the plants as well. It is like getting two birds with one stone or hitting a three-pointer while being fouled. You get a bonus. As the compost breaks down, nutrients move into the soil layer. Remember to layer the organic material 2 to 3 inches deep.

In colder climates, wait until early summer to add mulch. Do not mulch when the soil is still cool. Just because the frost date has passed and tomatoes are available in the garden centers does not mean conditions are ideal for growing veggies. Mulch, especially organic types, moderates soil temperatures. So if you mulch cool soil, it will stay cooler longer. Tomatoes grow best in warm (70 degrees F) soil so let the late spring sun heat the ground, then mulch.

To speed up the soil-warming process, you can cover your planting area with clear plastic in mid-spring. This traps enough of the sun's energy on the surface to warm the soil significantly. Remove the clear plastic when you plant.

Colored mulches have been tested for tomato productivity. Red seems to be the best color for increasing yields. Blue has shown good results too. The wavelengths reflected by the colors apparently speed ripening. There are conflicting studies, but if you are trying to improve your yield, it can't hurt.

Container gardeners should mulch too. The water-holding and temperature-moderating effects make a difference. Compost or worm casting are great choices because they feed as they mulch. Every time you water the containers, some nutrients will leach into the root zone. More decorative mulches for containers include pebbles, glass beads, sheet moss, Spanish moss, and reindeer moss.

A natural moss makes an effective mulch that does not float out of the pot in heavy rain or sprinkling.

My friend Sascha sent me several packs of SuperMoss (no relation) to experiment with last year. The reindeer moss was a hit. It conserved enough soil moisture that I gained one to two days between watering. Reindeer moss is ornamental and comes in several colors to match your color palette. More important, it's an effective mulch. The tomatoes seemed to love the reindeer moss. Fine roots grew right into the moss and anchored it down.

Crop Rotation

Despite the fun and ornamental value of container growing, tomatoes are best grown in the ground. The complex environment of good garden soil is impossible to duplicate in a container. Roots have much more space to spread out in the ground. The more widespread the roots, the more water and nutrients they are able to draw in for growth and production. The proof is in the plant. Tomatoes grown in the ground are often *twice* the size with more than *twice* the yield of container-grown plants. But in-ground tomatoes face more perils, especially if you don't practice crop rotation.

To get the most benefit out of in-ground planting, rotate your tomato crops. Don't plant them in the same space every year to avoid disease and nutrient problems. Pests and diseases from last season often survive in the soil over winter and attack similar crops. Diseases that attack tomatoes can affect eggplants, peppers, tomatillos, and other members of the nightshade family. It helps to plan a three- to four-year rotation with three to four crops in completely different families. For instance, the planting beds in my community garden are on an annual rotation between tomatoes, okra, beans, and pumpkins. Pick several unrelated plants to rotate with your tomatoes to keep your soil and crops healthy.

Plan a crop rotation for your containers too. Beans and sweet potatoes are good container crops to rotate with tomatoes. They help build the soil as they grow and leave it more fertile for your tomatoes. Alternatively, you can just dump last year's soil into the compost pile and add new soil mix.

Types of Tomatoes

Tomatoes have proven adaptable to nearly all climates. In fact, since they have been bred and grown in almost every corner of the world, you can find a productive variety regardless of your zone or location. In areas with short growing seasons and cool summers, varieties such as 'Stupice' and 'Early Girl' are good choices. In hot, humid areas that would stifle most tomatoes, 'Solar Set' and 'Tropic' excel. Unless you live on a mountaintop or in a pineapple under the sea, there's a tomato for you.

Indeterminate or Determinate

The growth of tomatoes is either indeterminate or determinate. Indeterminate tomatoes continue to grow throughout the growing season. There is theoretically no limit to their growth. Under ideal conditions (warm temperatures, adequate support, consistent fertilization, adequate water, and limited diseases and pests), indeterminate tomatoes should continue to grow and fruit forever.

When I first started growing tomatoes, this trait intrigued me. At the end of the season, I would bring in containers of tomatoes to see if I could keep them alive. They would last for a few weeks and then succumb to indoor conditions (inadequate light and dry air). Unless you have a greenhouse, let them die with dignity at first frost. Besides, bringing all that foliage and branches into the house is difficult and messy.

The lush, aggressive growth of indeterminate tomatoes is why the old wire tomato cages are rarely adequate. By late summer, indeterminate types are leafy beasts, completely overwhelming their cages and spilling out with axillary (nodes along the stem where leaves and branches emerge) clusters of fruit. The great benefit of the indeterminate tomatoes is the amount and duration of productivity. Besides the first fruit of the season, few things are appreciated more than a sun-ripened garden tomato picked at the end of the season in the crisp autumn air. Well-grown indeterminate tomatoes provide fruit from midseason until frost.

By contrast, determinate tomatoes have a predetermined growing limit. Like many nonvining annuals, they grow a set height and then begin to produce flowers all at once on terminal (tips of branches) clusters. Because of their limited growth, determinate tomatoes are popular as container plants and often are called patio or bush tomatoes. Many require only basic support and some of the more bushy types are self-supporting. After fruits are harvested, the plant loses vigor and begins to senesce (the process of dying).

Another characteristic of determinate tomatoes is that their fruits all ripen within a short period. For those making sauces or canning, this is ideal. You get a lot of ripe tomatoes when you need them. They will nearly all be at the perfect stage of readiness for preparation.

Not all determinates die back immediately after fruiting. Some, such as 'Czech's Bush', will produce a big crop and then slow down. The plant loses vitality, but doesn't die. These act like semideterminates. However, many gardeners treat them like determinates and replace them after the first big flush of fruiting.

The death of a determinant tomato plant after a big harvest is not necessarily a bad thing. It allows gardeners to replant the space with other veggies (called sucession planting). Most patio tomatoes finish in mid to late summer, allowing you to plant another quick crop, such as snow peas or field greens, before frost. In areas with long summers, you may be able to plant two crops of determinate tomatoes.

Determinate

Indeterminate

TOMATO TYPES

Determinate	Indeterminate
Smaller plant, controlled growth	Large plant, rampant growth
Ripens fruit early	Can ripen early to late
Ripens lots of fruit at once	Ripens fruit throughout the season
Dies back by midsummer	Grows and fruits until frost
Little to no staking	Requires strong supports
Veggie garden, flowerbeds	Veggie garden, back of borders
Great for containers	Okay in containers, bigger is better

Gardeners choose types of tomatoes based on their growing space and needs. If you only have a small space, then determinate tomatoes will fit the bill. Determinates are also a good choice if you need the bulk of your tomatoes at once for a canning project or farmers market. Indeterminates are for those who want tomatoes over a long season and have ample space. Also, when it comes to flavor, indeterminate tomatoes are judged to taste better. Often the best solution is to grow both kinds and get all the benefits.

More Tomato Types

Several categories describe the physical appearance of tomato fruits, including standard (or globe), beefsteak, oxheart, cherry, grape, and plum. Besides physical appearance, they differ in season and use.

Standard or globe tomatoes are the round ones you find in most stores. These medium-sized fruits are the literally the standards for the tomato industry. They are available year-round in grocery stores. When sliced, there is nearly an equal amount of meat and gel. You can use them for all your tomato needs.

Beefsteaks are the largest tomatoes. The wide, squat fruits can grow to 2 pounds or more. Beefsteaks have lots of flesh with small pockets of gel. When sliced, they resemble a marbled steak, hence the name. They have thin skin and don't ship well, so they are rarely offered in grocery stores (which is a good reason to grow them). Beefsteaks are the best for slicing on sandwiches and burgers because they are meaty and hold their shape well.

Oxhearts are similar to beefsteaks in all ways except shape. For those of you who don't regularly butcher an ox, it looks like a large strawberry. Oxhearts can rival beefsteaks in size, but typically have more gel pockets.

Cherry tomatoes include the really small but super prolific types. This is one of the few types that will actually produce in part shade. Most are about the size of their namesake, but they range smaller and larger. Cherries are typically early ripening, brightly colored, low in acid, juicy, and sweet. The plants can grow large, but are easy to maintain in the ground or in containers. These attributes make them good for school and children's gardens. Use them for salads, stir-fry dishes, and snacking in the garden.

Grape tomatoes resemble cherry tomatoes in size, but are more oblong like grapes. In productivity and sweetness, they are also similar to cherries. Unlike cherries they have more meat than juice and thick skins, so you occasionally find them in grocery stores. Grape types are fairly new to the market and have been bred with high disease resistance, heat tolerance, and productivity.

Plum or pear types are mid-sized and shaped like the fruits for which they are named. Both are meaty, dense tomatoes with thick skins and little to no pulp or seeds. The lack of juice allows them to quickly reduce down to sauce when cooked. Plum types are rarely eaten fresh. In fact this group is often referred to as paste tomatoes.

Tomato Heirlooms vs. Hybrids

Gardeners are choosing sides in this battle, but there is really no need for conflict. Heirloom and hybrid tomatoes compliment each other. You can grow both in your garden to get all the best benefits of tomatoes. The following chart shows the basic differences:

HEIRLOOM & HYBRID TOMATOES

Heirloom	Hybrid
Naturally pollinated	Scientifically bred
Good flavor	Variable flavor (good to bland)
Variable disease resistance	Good disease resistance
Variable productivity	High productivity
Variable ripening times	Earlier ripening times
Will produce a similar plant from its seed. Good for seed savers.	Will *not* produce a similar plant from its seed.
Good for home gardeners	Good for home gardeners and commercial production

Heirlooms

Heirloom or heritage tomatoes are literally heirlooms. Many are passed down through generations of tomato growers. It's similar to breeding dogs, cattle, or sheep. You only breed varieties that you like and hope the offspring have the same traits. Families would often save seeds of the best tasting or best cooking tomatoes. That is why heirlooms typically dominate the awards during taste tests. Most have effectively been bred for flavor.

Heirlooms are open pollinated. That means they are naturally pollinated without any formalized hybridizing or genetic modifications. The seeds from the fruits will contain many of the characteristics of the parent plant. Gardeners can exploit this by saving seeds from their best performing heirlooms. If you continue to sow the best seeds from the previous year and save seeds from the best plants of the current year, in theory you can create an heirloom that is acclimated to your garden's specific conditions. Over several generations, it may become unique enough to qualify as a new heirloom. But there are so many quality heirlooms on the market, that unless this becomes your passion, you can spend a lifetime just trying existing varieties.

Speeding the Heirloom Harvest

Some heirlooms are slow to mature and develop fruit. There are ways to increase productivity. Start with larger plants, provide adequate fertilizer, and harvest regularly. Starting with larger potted plants, if you can find transplants, shortens the time until the first harvest. Maintaining adequate nutrient levels prevents deficiencies, which can delay development. Harvesting regularly keeps the plant in full production. When you harvest a tomato, it sends a signal to the plant to produce more fruits. Pick heirloom tomatoes as soon as they are ripe.

Hybrids

Unlike heirlooms, which are typically bred by home gardeners, professional growers and companies raise hybrid tomatoes. Hybrids are bred mostly for commercial traits, such as productivity, early ripening, ability to transport, and disease resistance. Recently some of the newer hybrids, such as 'Biltmore', have been bred for taste too.

The hallmark of hybrids is that they are disease resistant. After the name of the hybrid varieties, there will be several letters. Those letters indicate the particular disease or pest for which the plant has resistance. Basically the more letters after the name, the better chance it has of combating diseases. Check with your local Extension Service to find out what diseases are prevalent in your area before buying your tomatoes. The following is a list of the letters with the corresponding pathogen.

A	Alternaria stem canker	**N**	Nematodes
F	Fusarium wilt race 1	**T**	Tobacco mosaic virus
FF	Fusarium wilt races 1 and 2	**St**	Stemphylium gray leaf spot
FFF	Fusarium wilt races 1, 2, and 3	**V**	Verticillium wilt

Hybrid crops represented a major breakthrough in agriculture. Prior to their use in the early part of the twentieth century, crop failure from disease was common. By the time you notice symptoms (discoloration, wilting despite adequate soil moisture, loss of vigor), it's too late. Diseases are easily spread from plant to plant through direct contact, soil splashing, insects, or unsterilized tools, such as pruners and shovels. Resistant varieties were a boon both for the agriculture industry and the home gardener.

The first filial generation, called F1 hybrids, is a cross from two distinctly different parents, like grolar bears (which are the offspring of a male grizzly and a female polar bear). Like grolars, F1 hybrid tomatoes can produce scion. But the offspring of F1 hybrids are not uniform and may not have the desired traits. What this means for gardeners is that you need to buy heirloom seed or plants to be sure to get the traits you want.

During fall cleanup, the occasional overripe tomato will drop to the ground and become covered with compost or mulch. Sometimes the seeds of those hybrid tomatoes survive and sprout in spring. When plants grow from seeds that the parent plant dropped the previous season, it is called a volunteer. As a novice gardener, I would let tomato volunteers grow in hopes of saving a few bucks. But only the heirlooms would come back true to their parents. The hybrids were completely different. Most of the volunteers from hybrids will revert to a generic, red cherry type. It is not a bad tomato, but it's *no* substitute for 'Early Girl', 'Celebrity', 'Sungold', or others.

Starting Tomatoes

Selecting Cell Packs and Potted Plants

Most people buy tomato seedlings in cell packs and pots and then transplant them into the garden. Regardless of the variety, check for stockiness, number of leaves, flowering/fruiting, disease, and pests when choosing tomatoes. Strong stocky plants with several sets of healthy-looking, pest-free, deep green leaves are your best bet. Reject anything that looks diseased, discolored, wilted, or infested. Tomatoes that are already flowering or fruiting are not preferred. Plants without flowers or fruit will recover from transplant shock faster in your garden. A quick recovery time means an earlier harvest time.

If all you can find are thin, lanky tomato seedlings, don't despair. Although it takes a little more work, legginess is not a big problem with tomatoes. You can plant the long stems under the ground. This is a no-no with most other plants. But tomato stems not only can survive under soil, but they can grow roots as well. (Even when planted totally aboveground, the lower portion of the stalk often grows knobby, adventitious roots.)

When you are planting, dig a deep hole and place the leggy seedling down in the hole with the top leaves 3 to 4 inches out of the ground. Remove any leaves along the stem that would be underground. Fill in around the plant with rich soil mix. The underground portion of the stem will begin to sprout new roots in a few days. For extra-long tomato seedlings, dig a trench and lay the plant down on its side. Angle the stem so that only the top leaves are above the soil. Prune off any leaves under the trench and then fill. You can lay several plants into a long trench. They can touch and overlap underground as long as there is consistent spacing above. This is the way to turn a floppy, lanky seedling into a well-anchored, stocky sprout. Since more roots equal more fruits, some growers always bury the tomato stems regardless of the plant's stockiness.

Sometimes you want to start with a larger tomato plant. For instance, many of the heirloom varieties develop slower and ripen later. Purchasing a larger plant reduces the number of days to first harvest and can make a big difference in your total yield. Fortunately, many good garden centers, such as my local Gethsemane Gardens, offer tomatoes in large pots by Mother's Day. In these cases it's okay to have flowers and fruit present. They cost a *bit* more than your standard cell pack of six, but the increased production can make it well worth the extra bucks. In colder climates, starting with larger plants can mean the difference between harvesting loads of sun-ripened fruit in late summer or scrambling to bring in loads of green tomatoes before the first fall frost.

Dig a shallow trench for planting extra-long seedlings.

Remember, you are gardening in a small space. You don't need a lot of tomato plants, which makes it easier to spend more per plant. Let's take the delicious and late-ripening 'Cherokee Purple' tomato for example. If you garden on a patio or in a small raised bed, you could buy a six-pack and then give away the five other seedlings that you don't need. Or you could buy one large plant in a 3-gallon container and then give away loads of delicious heirloom tomatoes a few months later. Your neighbors will be happier to receive your plump, heirloom tomatoes in August than they would have been with the puny seedlings in May. Plus giving away fresh-picked, homegrown veggies bolsters your garden reputation many more levels than store-bought seedlings. It's like the difference in giving someone a cup of flour today or a slice of cake next week.

Some gardeners like the experience of raising their veggies from seeds or seedlings to full grown and fruiting plants. However, it doesn't make you less of a gardener to start with larger, more developed plants. It's not cheating to let the professional growers do their thing. Small space gardeners need to use every advantage available to increase productivity.

Starting Seeds

Starting tomatoes from seeds requires more effort than buying potted plants, but seeds have some advantages, including variety, price, and cleanliness (free from diseases). Variety is the biggest benefit when growing from seed. You're lucky to find a dozen different types in the big stores. Even good garden centers typically offer only a couple dozen. Hundreds of varieties are available by seed that you will never find as a potted plant in any store. The different colors, flavors, shapes, sizes, and names are fascinating. Oftentimes, the hardest part of starting from seed is choosing which variety to grow. Order them so they arrive by early spring.

When you are ready to sow them, you will need a seedling tray or several pots. Lately I have been using plastic clamshells (you know, the plastic containers spinach, cashews, dried fruit, and such come in) as seed trays, instead of recycling them. Almost anything that holds soil and can drain excess water will do. Peat pots, egg cartons, yogurt cups, milk jugs, and so forth work well.

Use a seed germination mix or a light potting soil mix. You don't need any fertilizer now, but I do crush eggshells into the mix. Since this soil will ultimately be transplanted to the garden with the seedling, the eggshells provide extra calcium (necessary to fight blossom-end rot) throughout the season. Fill the containers a little more than halfway with soil mix. Sow the seeds and cover them with ⅛ inch of soil mix. Water carefully to avoid washing away seeds. After that, treat as any other indoor seedling.

Thin tomato seedlings so they are not touching. When each has two sets of leaves, you can transplant them into individual pots with a moist, sterile soil mix. Lift them carefully without crushing the stem or leaves. My favorite tools for handling seedlings are plastic takeout knives and forks. They are delicate on the roots but sturdy enough to get the job done. Get as much of the root system as possible.

Once potted, it is time to begin fertilizing the tomato seedlings. Use a water-soluble fertilizer at quarter strength for every watering. Gradually introduce the potted seedlings to outdoor conditions when all danger of frost has passed. Place them outside in part shade for a couple hours the first day. Increase that by one hour every day for several days, and move them into more sun. After the seedlings have been outside all day and their pots are full of roots, they are ready to be transplanted into the garden.

Although it is more involved than buying potted plants from a garden center, starting from seed is not difficult. One of my neighbors at my community garden, Pat, specializes in tomatoes and always starts from seed. For the last thirty-something years she has brought scores of her

THE COST OF GROWING TOMATOES

Start With	Price per Plant	17" Container and Inserts	Soil Amendments or Potting Mix
Seeds in-ground	$0.10	-	$6.00
Cell pack (6 total) in-ground	$0.50	-	$6.00
Gallon size in-ground	$5.00	-	$6.00
Gallon size in-container	$5.00	$45.00	$6.00
$64 Dollar Tomato	__.__	__.__	__.__

seedlings to the garden every spring. Her tomato plants are consistently among the biggest and first to flower. For the time-crunched, buying plants is the way to go, but if you have the time, it's a fun and rewarding process to try. Honestly, I find it easier to buy most of my plants, but when they finally create the 36-hour day, I'm going to go to all seeds like Pat.

The Myth of the $64 Tomato

The $64 Tomato is a hilarious book, but the author clearly needed some help. If he had had access to the *right* information (found in *this* book), he could have come out much better.

The average in-ground yield is about 10 pounds per plant or about 2 pounds per square foot. That's a very subjective amount and depends upon many factors, including tomato variety, soil type, watering, season length, and gardener expertise. Then sometimes there's no accounting for luck, good or bad. There are great seasons when I've harvested more than *30 pounds* from a 'Better Boy' tomato and some lousy ones when I've gotten only about 2 pounds from a 'Brandywine'. It is best to halve your harvest expectation for container growing. Let's say a very conservative 5 pounds per container, although large planters can be extremely productive. My Earth Box yielded more than 25 pounds of 'Super Snow White' one year.

Organic Fertilizer	Organic Pesticide and Fungicide	Total	Yield	Price per Tomato
$6.00	$10.00	$22.10	10	$2.21
$6.00	$10.00	$22.50	10	$2.25
$6.00	$10.00	$27.00	10	$2.70
$6.00	$10.00	$72.00	5	$14.40
___.___	___.___	___.___	1	$64.00

Tomato blossoms are a welcome sight and they signal that the first fruits of summer are not far away.

The table on the previous spread looks at the myth of the $64 tomato. This chart reflects an average gardener's work with one particular plant. For the sake of discussion and to compensate for variable rates of water usage, I erred on the high side and rounded all prices up. I also chose the most expensive materials. The seeds and plants are heirlooms, and the container is a 17-inch, tapered ornamental plastic composite with 12-inch Better Than Rocks inserts. Organic soil and fertilizers are included. To further slant the cost upward, let's assume that only 10 fruits were produced. For the container, we'll say only 5 fruits were produced.

The entire cost of all the materials was transferred to one plant to make a point. In practice, the costs would be spread over many plants and over many seasons. This is just an example to bust the myth.

You can see that even having to start from scratch with a new container and concentrating all the material costs on one plant will keep you well under $64 for one organically grown heirloom tomato. Stretched over more than one season you can eliminate most materials costs. If these were beefsteaks weighing about a pound each, that brings the price down to around fifty cents per pound of organic, heirloom tomatoes. What a bargain!

Problems

The majority of tomato problems are gardener inflicted. Tomatoes produce when they're given what they need. But like any crop, things can go wrong.

Little or no fruiting can happen for several reasons. Plants that suffer from lack of water, light, or nutrients may take longer to reach fruiting stage. Tomatoes fertilized with too much nitrogen may grow extra foliage and branches at the expense of flowers. If the plant is well developed and flowers but still does not fruit, then temperature may be the problem. Most tomatoes do not set fruit when day temps are consistently above 100 degrees F and night temps are above 75 degrees F. Gardeners in hot climates should choose heat-tolerant varieties acclimated to those conditions.

Blossom-end rot

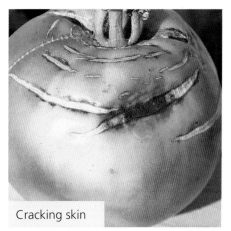
Cracking skin

Sun scald

Catfacing

Blossom-end rot (BER) is caused by an inability of tomato plants to absorb calcium. Symptoms show up in the fruit. The bottom (blossom end) of a tomato will turn black and sink into the fruit. Before the tomato ripens, rot will spread all across the bottom and render the tomato useless. BER is a frustrating condition because it can affect lots of tomatoes and it's avoidable. Often calcium is present in the soil, but the plant is unable to use it because the soil is too dry. Add supplemental calcium to the soil before planting and keep the soil moist.

Cracked or splitting skin is another condition caused by improper watering. If a fruiting plant is in dry soil, a big influx of water can cause cracked skin. During a heavy watering or rain, the roots draw in moisture for the parched plant. The fruits will expand from the water intake, but their skins can't expand quickly enough so they split. This is more prevalent among thin-skinned varieties. A consistent level of moisture prevents the plant from absorbing too big an influx of water for the fruits to contain. With even moisture, the skins on the fruits grow at a steady rate instead of starting and stopping, then splitting. If you can't water consistently, choose thick-skinned, crack-resistant varieties.

Sunscald is a condition that results from a tomato fruit's sudden exposure to direct, hot sunlight. The best prevention is to maintain healthy plants with good foliage. Limit pruning (except for diseased leaves) to provide some shade to maturing tomatoes.

Catfacing is a funny description that really does describe the appearance of an affected tomato. A tomato fruit will become gnarly and disfigured when some parts of it develop and others don't. Catfacing is caused by sudden drops of temperature (below 50 degrees F) as a plant is blooming or setting fruit. There's not much you can do to control Mother Nature, but if your plants are already outside, you can use row covers to protect them as much as possible. Of course, waiting to plant until all chances of cooler weather have passed is the best defense.

Pest Management

Tomato plants have few pests because they physically and chemically protect themselves against being eaten. The leaves are covered in tiny, fuzzy

Tomato hornworm

hairs that serve as a barrier to the tender leaves. The foliage and stems contain a mild toxin to discourage feeding. But there are a few common pests that can break through a tomato's defenses.

Monitoring is most crucial part of any pest management program. Check your plants when you water, harvest, or walk by. Pollinators and good bugs will be on top of the leaves and flowers.

Aphids like to hide themselves and their eggs under the leaves, so be sure to turn them over and look for them. Other pests will be clearly visible.

Tomato and tobacco hornworms both love tomatoes. These are big caterpillars that cause noticeable damage. Their fearsome looking horn is a bluff. Hornworms are harmless unless you are tomato foliage. If you have them, you will literally see the leaves disappearing before your eyes. These finger-sized tomato munchers are the larvae of the beautiful and fast-flying hawk and sphinx moths. The caterpillars do major damage to plants and even eat green tomatoes. In contrast with aphids, hornworm problems are common in more natural areas and rare in isolated gardens. I seem to have hornworms every other year in my community garden plot, but they have never been seen on my balcony or rooftop.

Beneficial biologicals work well on tomato pests. Ladybugs devour aphids. Tiny braconid wasps use hornworms to nurture their young. Adult females insert eggs into hornworms. After hatching, the wasp larvae literally eat the hornworms alive from the inside. It's like watching an *Aliens* movie in the veggie garden. You can buy the braconid wasps, but if you have enough hornworms, the wasps find them on their own. As the larvae feed, the worm moves slower. When the young wasps emerge from their cocoons and fly away, all that's left of the hornworm is a sad sack of skin. *Bacillus thuringiensis*, B.t., is beneficial bacteria (sold as a powder) that is much less graphic and stops caterpillar feeding by giving them a tummy ache.

Use mechanical methods of control (handpicking, crushing, washing off) as well. If things get out of hand, look for chemical solutions. Again, try to choose products listed by the OMRI or USDA for organic gardening. Studies have shown links between ADHD in kids and pesticide ingestion.

Powdery mildew and other fungal diseases can affect tomato foliage. Apply a fungicide to stop the spread, but it is much better to avoid the disease altogether. To discourage fungi, water the root zone, not the leaves. Healthy tomatoes can fight against pests and diseases. Look for resistant varieties. Prepare the space before planting. Give them proper sunlight, water, soil, and nutrients, and you'll have fewer problems.

Tomatoes in the Kitchen

The versatility of tomatoes in the kitchen adds to their popularity. Tomatoes are eaten fresh, in salads, sliced, and cooked in myriad dishes. Roasting or stir-frying lessens their acidity and enhances their sweetness. Tomatoes are part of many of our favorite recipes from all over the world. Try to imagine Italian, Mexican, or Senegalese cuisine without tomatoes. Plus, they can be dried, canned, or sauced, providing a way to preserve the taste of summer for the rest of the year.

Green (Unripe) Tomatoes

Tomatoes produce food over a long season. You can begin harvesting when they are green. Green tomatoes cannot be eaten raw, but you can cook or pickle them. If you have an abundance of immature fruits early in the season, fry up green tomatoes or prepare them into a chow-chow. Do you wait for them to ripen or use them green? This is always a tough decision. The largest green ones are the best for cooking, but they are also the closest to actually ripening. Sometimes the choice is decided by the variety. It is better to take a few green tomatoes from early-ripening, highly productive types than late-ripening, low-yield ones.

Before frost, harvest all your tomatoes. You can pick them individually or just cut the whole plant. You have two options with the green ones: prepare them or allow them to ripen. If you choose to ripen them, keep them away from direct sunlight and hot or cold temperatures. Like you, tomatoes are comfortable at room temperature. Despite common practice, they should not go in the windowsill. Place them in a paper bag or between sheets of newspaper. Put an apple in the bag with them to hasten ripening. Check every week for ripe ones. It's a distant second to vine ripening in taste and appearance, but much better than letting frost get them.

More Tomato Tips & Techniques

Because tomatoes are loaded with vitamins and minerals—including lycopene, a powerful antioxidant shown to combat cancer—people of all ages can benefit from eating more tomatoes.

For kids, choose snacking tomatoes that are bite-sized, colorful, and sweet, like 'Sungold'. For pizza-themed gardens, plant paste tomatoes. When working with kids, always select those types that resist diseases, are early ripening, and have high productivity to ensure success. Add herbs such as oregano or rosemary as companion plants to help deter pests and season tasty dishes. Children develop habits early, so make gardening and harvesting fresh food a pleasant part of their daily routine.

For all you newbies, there are two mantras to keep in mind:

1. **Start small so it stays manageable.** Families gardening for the first time should start with a small plot, a 8 × 4-foot raised bed, or a few containers. Remember, 10 tomato plants is 5 too many for most new gardeners.

2. **Have fun.** If you ever feel stressed about your tomato plants or garden in general—stop. Find a seat in the shade, take a few breaths, and watch the clouds go by. Give yourself time to regroup. Play a game with the kids. Your tomatoes will be fine. If not, like the Chicago Cubs, there's always next year.

Chapter 6

TOP TOMATO PICKS

THIS LIST INCLUDES SOME OF THE BEST tomatoes for small space gardens. They are not all small plants, but they are all tasty, adaptable, and easy to grow. Most of them have similar requirements for successful growth, such as:

* **Water:** Mesic or medium moisture; don't allow soil to dry out completely between watering. Water the base of plants.

* **Fertilizer:** Apply when planting, as plants begin to flower, and every three weeks after that. Use a complete, calcium-rich fertilizer to reduce blossom-end rot. Stop fertilizing a month before the season ends.

* **Uses:** With the exception of 'San Marzano', the selected tomatoes are delicious sliced fresh on a plate or in salads, and all of them can be roasted, sauced, and cooked in recipes. Roasting intensifies the flavor and seems to add sweetness even to acidic tomatoes.

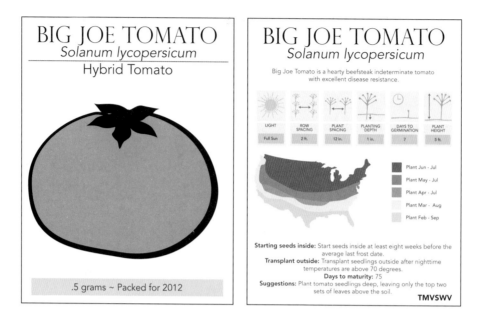

BIG JOE TOMATO
Solanum lycopersicum
Hybrid Tomato

.5 grams ~ Packed for 2012

BIG JOE TOMATO
Solanum lycopersicum

Big Joe Tomato is a hearty beefsteak indeterminate tomato with excellent disease resistance.

LIGHT	ROW SPACING	PLANT SPACING	PLANTING DEPTH	DAYS TO GERMINATION	PLANT HEIGHT
Full Sun	2 ft.	12 in.	1 in.	7	5 ft.

Plant Jun - Jul
Plant May - Jul
Plant Apr - Jul
Plant Mar - Aug
Plant Feb - Sep

Starting seeds inside: Start seeds inside at least eight weeks before the average last frost date.
Transplant outside: Transplant seedlings outside after nighttime temperatures are above 70 degrees.
Days to maturity: 75
Suggestions: Plant tomato seedlings deep, leaving only the top two sets of leaves above the soil.

TMVSWV

Of course there are differences in the tomatoes, which are explained in the following categories.

Type & Culture describes the tomato and how to care for it. This category will detail:
* heirloom or hybrid type
* weight range of typical fruit
* where it can be planted
* special care conditions

Plant Size covers the following:
* Determinate (smaller plants that stop growing when they set fruit and may die after ripening the tomatoes) and indeterminate (larger plants that continue to grow throughout the season as they set and ripen fruit). Semideterminate plants behave mostly like determinates but continue to grow and produce after the first big flush of fruit.
* The average height of a plant grown under ideal garden conditions (full sun, rich soil, adequate water). With a little luck, they can grow larger. Plants grown in containers and hanging baskets will be smaller.

Bears Fruit Within covers the average number of days from transplanting to first ripe fruit.

Biltmore VFFASt

This bright red hybrid tomato is tough, tasty, and especially good for new gardeners.

Like most modern hybrids, 'Biltmore' has been bred for early maturity and disease resistance. However, it also has a rich, meaty flavor. 'Biltmore' has even won taste contests against champion heirloom varieties, such as 'Cherokee Purple' and 'Brandywine'.

Type & Culture: hybrid, 8- to 12-ounce standard globe tomato; use in the ground and in containers

Plant Size: determinate, 6 feet

Bears Fruit Within: 70 days, midseason

'Biltmore' loads itself with clusters of medium tomatoes. Their uniform size and bright red color make them appealing for the home and market gardener. Because of their thicker skin, 'Biltmore' tomatoes crack less and travel well. A determinate type, they ripen a lot of fruit at once, giving you plenty for canning, sharing, or selling.

'Biltmore' has strong disease resistance to many of the worst offenders. Because a good crop is virtually assured (knock on wood to avoid jinxes), 'Biltmore' is a smart choice for professional growers and beginners. The flavorful pulp makes it a good choice for chefs and gourmets. With a large number of fruits ripening at once, this is a fine pick for canners too.

The determinate growth of 'Biltmore' allows it to grow well in containers and in small gardens. They love open space, but feel free to tuck them into a perennial border or flowerbed. It's an attractive plant with stout branches. Hold the tomatoes at an angle for easy picking. These lush, tough, productive tomatoes are gaining popularity. With all their attributes, 'Biltmore' tomatoes can be a winner for any garden. Now if only there were garden gnomes to help with the canning.

Cherokee Purple

An award-winning tomato with rich flavors and colors.

These were originally cultivated by a Cherokee tribe in Tennessee, which explains part of the name. The "Purple" part is more confusing because the actual color is more of a blend of pink, mauve, rust, slate, and taupe with olive green shoulders. Fortunately, someone with more marketing sense than me chose 'Cherokee Purple'. Cherokee Pinkish Mauvish Taupe just doesn't sing.

Type & Culture: heirloom, 4- to 16-ounce flattened globe tomato; in the ground and in containers. Water regularly to limit the fruit from cracking (some cracking is expected, especially after heavy rains).

Plant Size: indeterminate, large at about 6 feet tall or more

Bears Fruit Within: 80 days, late season

'Cherokee Purple' has reached cult status among tomato growers. Its medium-sized fruits are filled with a flavor as smoky and multihued as the Appalachian hills where it originated. Fortunately for gardeners, this award winner is one of the heirlooms most commonly available in garden centers and stores.

'Cherokee Purple' tomatoes like warm weather. Here in Chicago they are slow growers through early summer. Then once it's hot, they explode in lush growth and blooms. By early fall, fruits are ripening. To increase production, start with larger plants and place in a warm, sheltered spot.

These require sturdy staking. The rangy branches will bend without adequate support for the fruit. The dusky fruits aren't the most attractive of the tomato clan, but thankfully, the splits, lumps, and cat facing don't affect the savory flavor. Harvest when the tomato's shoulders are still green. If you wait until the shoulders turn deep pink, the tomato will be overripe and mushy. Pick them when they begin feel soft and the bottom is a purplish color.

If you've got the space to grow several tomatoes, definitely include 'Cherokee Purple' in the mix. It consistently finishes among the top in taste tests with many gardeners who claim it's the best they have ever tried. For a dynamic summer treat, slice up a couple on a plate with a side of crunchy roasted okra hot from the oven and some sea salt . . . delicious!

Czech's Bush

Productive, compact bright red bush tomato especially suited for containers and tight spaces.

'Czech's Bush' makes this list for its small, sturdy stature and productivity. This heirloom originated in Czechoslovakia where it has been grown for generations. It made the journey to America in the late 1970s and has been producing heavily in pots and small gardens ever since.

Type & Culture: heirloom, 3- to 6-ounce standard globe tomato; in the ground,
    containers, and hanging pots. Water regularly to prevent cracking.

Plant Size: determinate, compact at about 3 feet tall

Bears Fruit Within: 65 days, midseason

'Czech's Bush' tomatoes have a stocky nature that makes them perfect for container gardening. A 16-inch container and a couple of 3-foot-tall bamboo stakes are all you need. Loosely attach the main stems to a support. The plant won't outgrow the container, and you don't have to continually adjust the ties and stakes like you would for other tomatoes.

'Czech's Bush' is a well-behaved plant with thick, ornamental, dark green foliage. Masses of lemon yellow flowers are followed by clusters of pink tomatoes after about eight weeks. Although listed as a determinate type, semideterminate is a better description. 'Czech's Bush' tomato plants produce a lot of fruit at once, but do not die after ripening, like a typical determinate. They lose vigor and drop some leaves, but they continue to produce some tomatoes until frost.

With the majority of its fruits ripening at once, 'Czech's Bush' is good for canning and recipes that require a lot of tomatoes. They are the perfect size for quartering in salads. Since it has a lot of pulp and juice, 'Czech's Bush' is one of our favorites to roast with fresh herbs.

Early Girl VFF

A popular early-ripening red tomato.

'Early Girl' popularity is directly related to its early bearing habit. For gardeners with short seasons in cold climates or high altitudes, this may be the most productive choice.

Type & Culture: hybrid, 4- to 8-ounce standard globe tomato; in the ground, containers, and hanging baskets. Drought resistant once established.

Plant Size: indeterminate, about 6 feet tall or more

Bears Fruit Within: 52 days, early season

'Early Girl' is one of the first tomatoes I ever grew. The name's promise was all I needed. This is one of the most popular varieties, and you will find it wherever tomatoes are sold. An 'Early Girl' tomato's productivity, uniformity, and disease resistance (against verticillium and fusarium wilts 1 and 2) are other hallmarks of this reliable hybrid.

Staking is necessary and ongoing, as this vigorous tomato continues to grow and fruit until frost. It is not uncommon for a well-fed 'Early Girl' to reach over 8 feet high and provide scores of bright red, 6-ounce tomatoes. To get the most production, you will have to water and feed regularly. But this is one tomato that you don't have to coddle.

Some gardeners out West use 'Early Girl' for dry farming. Basically, they water transplants sparingly or not at all to force the roots deep into the clay soil for moisture. The plants are much smaller and much less productive, but dry-farmed 'Early Girl' tomatoes are said to rival the best heirlooms in taste tests.

Gardeners with short summers can get a good harvest with 'Early Girl'. This is the first slicing tomato to ripen. During the early part of summer, they are the only big game in town, so we use them for everything. Later in the season, as larger and tastier tomatoes begin to ripen, 'Early Girl' tomatoes are still appreciated but relegated to recipes, canning, and sharing.

Garden Peach

Fuzzy, pinkish yellow tomatoes with a mild, sweet taste are an interesting treat. It's *fuzzy*! Really. Its suede-like skin makes 'Garden Peach' a unique tomato in the garden. The skin is actually thin, but the fuzz adds interesting texture, especially when you pop the whole thing in your mouth.

Type & Culture: heirloom, 2- to 4-ounce standard globe tomato; in the ground, containers, and hanging baskets

Plant Size: indeterminate, about 5 feet tall

Bears Fruit Within: 80 days, late season

Besides the name, 'Garden Peach' shares the shape and coloration of a true peach. Both fruits are also sweet and juicy. It may not be as sweet and succulent as a fresh-picked Carolina peach, but a well-grown 'Garden Peach' tomato tastes better than some of the bland, mushy, store-bought peaches I've tried.

To be an ancient heirloom from Peru, it's surprisingly vigorous and disease resistant. The plant produces heavily and grows well, so staking is necessary. Well-tended plants can grow over 8 feet tall and produce scores of fruit late in the season. The fuzzy skin seems to help preserve a 'Garden Peach' tomato's shelf life. It's not uncommon for 'Garden Peach' tomatoes to keep for several months after harvesting.

Although a novelty for its fuzz, 'Garden Peach' is a quality eating tomato. The snack-sized fruits taste mild and sweet with a low acid pulp. Those who don't like the texture can just peel the skin away. 'Garden Peach' can be prepared in numerous ways, but to appreciate its extraordinary qualities, serve them whole and fuzzy. Place in a red or bright green dish for edible art that's also a nutritious conversation piece.

Jet Star VF

This productive, bright red hybrid with vigorous plants and great taste was bred for northern growers but excels in many parts of the country.

'Jet Star' breeders set out to produce a plant with loads of beautiful, tasty, low-maintenance tomatoes. They succeeded. The bright red to orange-red, flavorful, plentiful ½-pound tomatoes are picture perfect.

Type & Culture: hybrid, 6- to 12-ounce standard globe tomato; in the ground and in containers

Plant Size: indeterminate, somewhat compact, about 5 feet tall

Bears Fruit Within: 70 days, midseason

'Jet Star' tomatoes have a uniform appearance and are crack resistant, so they rarely split—even after heavy downpours. This makes them exquisite market tomatoes. Combine that with their high productivity and disease resistance and it's easy to see why 'Jet Star' has been a favorite of professional growers and markets since its introduction in 1969.

I finally grew 'Jet Star' in a well-amended veggie garden at my ma's last year. Despite being listed as a compact variety around 5 feet tall, the

vigorous plants grew over 7 feet tall and had to be staked both upward and outward several times. 'Jet Star' produces continually, but the lush foliage can hide ripe tomatoes. Every few days go on a detailed treasure hunt for ripe ones. The tomatoes are typically about 8 ounces, but there were a couple of monsters over 1 pound.

You will have to give these tomatoes good support. Besides tying and staking, 'Jet Star' is super easy to grow. It is disease resistant and heat tolerant. Mr. Vowels, a garden colleague's father and professional tomato grower from Kentucky, has grown 'Jet Star' for thirty years and claims it is still among his top three varieties in production and demand. Some growers have switched to the newer, larger-fruited, more resistant 'Jetsetter', but 'Jet Star' is still a fan favorite.

Even though 'Jet Star' is a midsized standard tomato, it cuts like a beefsteak. The network of meaty flesh pocketed with gel-like pulp holds its shape when sliced. The flavor is mild and slightly sweet with low acidity. This is a good general tomato to have handy for salads, sandwiches, and next-door neighbors.

Pink Oxheart

Huge bright pink tomatoes on prolific vines are sure to please your taste buds. 'Pink Oxheart' is a tomato lover's dream. These big, beautiful, heart-shaped tomatoes have a meaty flesh with rich flavor. Their sheer size is enough to make gardeners smile.

Type & Culture: heirloom, 1 pound oxheart tomato; in the ground and in large containers

Plant Size: indeterminate, large at around 6 feet tall or more

Bears Fruit Within: 80 days, late season

I typically grow medium-sized tomatoes on my rooftop because of the strong winds and exposure. 'Pink Oxheart' tomatoes' tough constitution can withstand those conditions, although the fruits are a little smaller than the hefty 1-pounders you get from a sheltered location.

Gardeners need strong support systems to hold 'Pink Oxheart'. Unlike some other oxhearts, these Hungarian heirlooms have high yields. Sturdy stakes or modular cages are needed for the vigorous vines and large fruits. Attach ties near the base of tomato clusters to prevent branches from bending under the weight.

My friend Patti grows 'Pink Oxheart' tomatoes in her inner-city Boston garden. Her plants are nearly 8 feet tall and loaded with fruit from summer to fall. Her compost and rabbit manure soil mixture produces monster fruit. Some of the 2 pounders are big enough that you need both hands to hold them.

'Pink Oxheart' tomatoes are the right size and texture for burgers and sandwiches, but you can use them for anything. The pulp is sweet and there are few seeds. Patti and I sliced up a couple right in the garden. Patti picked basil leaves to eat with hers. I seasoned my slices with some tangy, crisp arugula and salt. If you are a fan of meaty tomatoes, definitely make a space for 'Pink Oxheart'.

San Marzano

This deep red tomato is the one lauded by culinary community for authentic sauces and tomato paste.

This Italian heirloom's ancestor is reported to have come from Peru. Through generations of cultivation in rich, volcanic soil and warm Neapolitan sunshine, 'San Marzano' was created.

Type & Culture: heirloom, paste (or plum) tomato; in the ground, containers, and hanging pots

Plant Size: indeterminate, around 6 feet tall

Bears Fruit Within: 80 days, late season

'San Marzano' is the most sought-after paste tomato in the world. Top chefs everywhere swear by its authentic flavor. Canned 'San Marzano' tomatoes and sauces are gourmet items. More than 80,000 tons of 'San Marzano' tomatoes are exported from the Campania region of Italy annually. It is such a big business that scientists use DNA techniques to ensure that the exported cans of sauce are actually 'San Marzano' fruits.

The thin-skinned 4-ounce fruits with little pulp, few seeds, low acid, and low sugar are perfect for sauces. Drying intensifies the flavor. Unlike many other plum tomatoes, 'San Marzano' is indeterminate and produces clusters of oblong tomatoes until frost. There are typically 10 to 12 clusters of five to six tomatoes per season. You need to stake the vines, but since it is not a rampant grower that is not difficult. The plant needs plenty of space and sun to produce maximum yields. This is one that you don't want to crowd. Let every tomato have a chance at sunlight.

I'm a fan of *Lidia's Italy* cooking show on PBS. Lidia said 'San Marzano' was her favorite tomato, so I had to grow it. I definitely understand why chefs love it. But gardeners should note that this is a tomato for sauce or drying. It's fantastic in a meat sauce or on pasta dish, but not so much for slicing or salads.

Sungold FT

Sungold's beautiful yellow-orange to deep orange tomatoes are like eating sweet juicy sunshine.

For gardeners, they are a dream. Beginners should start with this variety if they want guaranteed success. This hybrid resists disease, fruits early, and yields heavily. I don't remember ever having major problems with 'Sungold'.

Type & Culture: hybrid, ¼- to ½-ounce cherry tomato; in the ground,
   in containers, and hanging pots

Plant Size: indeterminate, 6 feet tall or more

Bears Fruit Within: 55 days, early season

'Sungold' is the only tomato I'm mandated to grow every year. My wife demands *at least* one 'Sungold' container on the rooftop so she can snack on them. Everyone who tries 'Sungold' loves them. Because they are so fruity and sweet, even kids can be fooled into eating healthy.

They always produce a multitude of sweet tomato clusters. 'Sungold' tomatoes excel in containers, small spaces, urban environments, and hanging pots. You can grow them in the North, South, East, or West. Full sun is the only thing necessary for the sweetest fruits. They are forgiving of almost everything else, including neglect. Of course, regular watering and staking helps production. Fortunately staking is simple because the branches are flexible and the fruit is light.

The fruity taste and firm flesh drive the popularity of these. My favorite way to eat 'Sungold' is fresh from the garden. In salads they are so sweet and tangy that you don't need cranberries or raisins. They also cook well and make great additions to stir-fry dishes and omelettes.

'Sungold' produces heavily right up until frost. However, late in the season there is not enough sun or heat for it to produce as many sugars, so in fall roast them to intensify their flavor and sweetness.

Sunset's Red Horizon (aka Rostova)

One of the biggest, best-tasting tomatoes available.

The size alone is a selling point. The Russian name translates into "red giant of Rostov." The grapefruit-sized tomatoes are stunning on the vine and incredible on the table.

Type & Culture: heirloom, oxheart tomato; in the ground and in containers

Plant Size: indeterminate, 8 feet tall

Bears Fruit Within: 72 days, midseason

'Sunset's Red Horizon' is listed here because my sister Teresa grew it and raved about its size, productivity, and taste. Everyone who sampled the fleshy, fruity tomatoes said 'Sunset's Red Horizon' tomatoes were the best they had ever tasted. It's hard to disagree. This beefsteak has firm, meaty flesh and sugary pulp with low acid. It reminds me of the sweet layer right before you get to the rind of a honeydew melon.

You'll have to stake them and continually support the heavy fruit; otherwise, these are easy to grow. Although an heirloom, 'Sunset's Red Horizon' has good disease resistance, sets fruit in cold weather, resists cracking, and rarely suffers blossom-end rot. It's a prolific plant that produces large, bright tomatoes up to hard frost. Once you grow this tomato, you will understand why 'Sunset's Red Horizon' is gaining worldwide popularity.

Teresa ate most of hers fresh from the garden, like an apple. You don't even need salt. Although they can be prepared like any other tomato, the thin skin, meaty

flesh, and sweet juice proved too tempting for my family. None of the prolific crop survived the walk to the kitchen. I advise growing a couple of plants to accommodate snacking and cooking.

Super Snow White

This is a good snacking tomato that offers unique color in the garden and on the plate. Fruits are faded ivory, changing to pale yellow the more they ripen. This tomato was a surprise to me. I've heard negative things about white tomatoes, but it performed well and was flavorful. The tomatoes remain ivory to pale yellow after cooking, which makes for some tasty confuse-your-friends-type dishes, such as pasta with ivory tomato sauce.

Type & Culture: heirloom, 1- to 2-ounce cherry tomato; in the ground, containers, and hanging pots. Water regularly to prevent fruit from cracking.

Plant Size: indeterminate, around 6 feet tall

Bears Fruit Within: 70 days, midseason

'Super Snow White' is classified as a cherry tomato; however, it is much larger than 'Tommy Toe' or 'Sungold'. In ideal conditions the snack-sized fruits keep growing, and I've had some big ones closer to 3 ounces.

This is a fun tomato to grow, especially for kids. Its cartoon name, small size, and unusual color make them perfect for children's gardens or kids' containers. 'Super Snow White' requires strong support for its prolific, colorful clusters, produced all season. Other than staking, this is an easy-to-grow, productive, disease-resistant, sweet tomato that's sure to please.

I grew 'Super Snow White' in an Earth Box last year. In a two-week period in September, I harvested more than 120 tomatoes! In-ground plantings are even more productive and plants typically grow more than 6 feet tall.

Use 'Super Snow White' for salads, recipes, and sauces. It is a great tomato for snacking right in the garden with plenty left to harvest. The flesh is firm and there's lots of sweet juice. Although technically not a low-acid type, the sweetness of the pulp surpasses the acidity, giving this healthy treat a mild, pleasant flavor.

Top Ten Veggies for Small Spaces

1 Bush cucumber

2 Carrot

3 Climbing squash

4 Leaf lettuce

5 Onion

6 Peas

7 Cherry tomato

8 Pole beans

9 Potato

10 Sweet pepper

Veggies for Special Sites

Veggies make gardening more rewarding. Producing your own food (even if limited in variety or amount) lifts the spirits and encourages the soul. On the practical side, growing some crops boosts your nutrition, sharpens culinary skills, and gets you outdoors.

Many of us can't expect to be self-sufficient with our gardening. That's okay. We all enjoy visiting the friendly folks at the farmers market. But sometimes you need a sprig of fresh parsley, some lettuce, or a vine-ripe tomato. That's when a veggie garden can save the day. Whether you have a backyard plot or just a few balcony containers, these plants will perform. This list features some tasty, nutritious crops that will grow right outside your kitchen door.

To grow vegetables in a small space requires careful planning and preparation. Prepare a well-drained, fertile soil by amending with lots of organic matter and a slow-release fertilizer before planting. Use a balanced fertilizer when planting and add organic topdressing in early summer. You have to sow cool-season crops early. As summer approaches, cool-season crops need to be harvested, so you can plant warm-season veggies.

Bush cucumbers are a good option for small spaces. These compact plants stand about 2 feet tall with an equal spread. They require an open space with air circulation for good production. Don't crowd the plants. Harvest cucumbers when they are small for best taste and texture. Frequent harvesting signals the plant to produce more cucumbers.

VEGGIES FOR SMALL SPACES

Plant	Minimal Space Needed	Place	Shade Tolerant	Season
Bush cucumber	4 sq. ft.	Small yard, community plot, large container	No	Warm
Carrot	8 per sq. ft.	Small yard, community plot, large container	No	Cool
Climbing squash	4 sq. ft.	Small yard, community plot, large container	No	Warm
Leaf lettuce	4 per sq. ft.	Small yard, community plot, container	Yes	Cool
Onion	6 per sq. ft.	Small yard, community plot, large container	No	Cool
Patio tomato	4 sq. ft.	Small yard, community plot, large container	No	Warm
Peas	8 per sq. ft.	Small yard, community plot, large container	No	Cool
Pole bean	8 per sq. ft.	Small yard, community plot, large container	No	Warm
Potato	4 sq. ft.	Small yard, community plot, large container	No	Cool
Sweet pepper	4 sq. ft.	Small yard, community plot, large container	No	Warm

Cucumber blossom

Carrots are easy to grow from seeds. Make sure the soil is deep. Succession planting works well for carrots; sow some seeds every three weeks from mid-spring through early summer. With the right varieties, you can have garden-fresh carrots all season. Harvest carrots when they are small— 2 inches in diameter. This ensures that they will be sweet and tender.

Climbing squash are the only types recommended for small gardens. Squash can be large and rambling. Train them on a trellis to keep the plant manageable and make picking easy. Place in the back of beds or use as screening. Give plants open space with good air circulation. The more squash you harvest, the more it will produce.

Leaf lettuces are one of the first crops ready in spring. They can also be sown again in late summer for a fall crop. You can buy specific lettuce seeds or buy a field greens mix that will have other greens included. The field green mixes usually contain a blend of colorful salad greens. Besides being ornamental and tasty, field greens provide early-season vitamins, minerals, and fiber. To extend the harvest, take individual leaves instead of the whole plant. Warm weather causes the leaves to become bitter, so harvest entire plants beginning in late spring.

Onions can be sown as early as late winter. These cold-hardy bulbs need regular watering during hot, dry weather to keep actively growing. Remove and discard any bulbs that show disease. Snap off any flowers that begin to form. The *Allium* clan is loaded with ornamental members, but you want your garden onion for the plump, zesty bulb, not the flowers.

Patio tomatoes are suited for small gardens. Cherry and other small tomatoes grow fast and can ramble over other plants, so they are great for tight spots. Tie to them to a trellis or other support to keep them upright. They are the only type of tomato that can produce a decent crop in partial shade.

Peas are perfect for vertical gardening. Train them on a trellis. They are an ornamental plant with decorative foliage and butterfly-like flowers. Harvest tender pods of sugar snap peas and snow peas when the peas inside are still small. Although you can harvest English peas at the same stage, it is best to let the peas inside the pods swell. At full ripeness, English pea pods will be tough and inedible, but the peas inside will be succulent and sweet.

Pole beans are another candidate for vertical gardening. They can grow over 10 feet, so gardeners often use big trellises or tie together long bamboo canes to form bean teepees. The teepees are more decorative and sturdier than a single row of poles. Pinch the tips of the growing stems when pole bean vines are 5 feet tall to keep the pods within reach. Pole beans may stop producing after a few harvests. Don't hesitate to cut them down and plant a fall crop.

Potatoes need sunny spaces with a deep, rich soil. Mulch plants one week after they sprout and keep a thick layer of mulch on them throughout the season. The mulch layer keeps the soil cooler, conserves soil moisture, and suppresses weeds. The mulch also acts as a covering to keep developing potatoes in the dark. If sunlight hits the potatoes, they will turn green and become inedible. Plant potatoes in succession for an extended harvest. The foliage and flowers are ornamental in the garden.

Sweet peppers do double duty as ornamental edibles in the garden, which makes them perfect for small spaces. The colorful bells and cones decorate the veggie garden. A well-grown pepper can look like a bushy Christmas tree with ornaments. Fruits come in a vast color range. They start green and slowly turn yellow, orange, red, and/or deep purple. Some go directly from green to their ripe color. Other varieties meander through a spectrum before ripening and sweetening. Place peppers in the front of your garden where you can admire them and easily harvest them.

Your typical 'California Wonder' sweet pepper is a good producer, but may ripen too slowly in colder climates. Those with shorter summers should look into 'Gypsy' and 'Carmen' sweet peppers. These hybrids are prolific even in containers. 'Gypsy' grows into a compact plant loaded with greenish ivory fruits shaped like small bell peppers. 'Carmen' produces heavily on a larger plant with conical, green fruits. Both ripen to a deep, bright red with crisp mild flavor.

Top Ten Edibles for Containers

1 Bush beans

2 Chili pepper

3 Kale

4 Lemon thyme

5 Marjoram

6 Mustard greens

7 Patio tomato

8 Radish

9 Serviceberry 'Regent'

10 Sweet potato

These plants produce better than most in containers and don't require much care. With the exception of the bush beans, they are drought tolerant. Of course, the more water you give them, the more productive they are. But their tough constitution means you can go on vacation with no worries. The lemon thyme and serviceberry are hardy enough to stay outside in their containers year-round.

Bush beans can be planted in containers because they don't require much staking and they ripen fast. I can't always get to my community garden every day. The beans need to be closer (right outside my door) if I'm going to pick them at the young, tender, gourmet, can-eat-them-raw stage. On top of that, there are fewer pests (grasshoppers, cucumber beetles, and so forth) on my rooftop than at the community plot. Bush beans have the extra benefit of adding nitrogen to the soil, which helps the next crop planted in the pot.

Chili peppers are often the most ornamental plant in the garden. The chilies ripen at different times, producing a kaleidoscope of colors. Plant them in something decorative that complements their beauty. Set the container in a spot where you can admire it. When dining outside, place the pot on the table as an edible and spicy centerpiece.

Kale has a combination of ornament and texture that makes for an exceptional container plant. You can harvest the leaves a few at a time throughout the season or, depending on your need, take them all at once and plant another. Group pots of kale with pots of bright flowers for decoration, contrast, and interest. 'Russian Red' and 'Toscano' are good varieties for beauty and eating.

Lemon thyme is a hardy, low-growing, aromatic groundcover. Bright purple flowers cover the plant in summer. Besides being a beautiful, easy-to-grow plant, it is also a valued culinary herb. Lemon thyme seasons poultry and fish dishes with a citrusy, savory taste. And it's drought tolerant. It works in Zones 4 to 9.

Marjoram is the underused sibling of oregano. It fills containers with super fragrant, hoary green foliage. Cut the white flowers off to get more leaves, or allow them to bloom and attract pollinators. Marjoram leaves are strong flavored, and it only takes a few to flavor dishes. Before frost, cut all stems and bring inside to dry for use throughout winter.

Mizuna mustard is an underrated salad green. You can grow and harvest it all season. Unlike other greens, it doesn't get bitter in the summer. With its glossy, deeply lobed leaves, mizuna makes an attractive potted plant. Use the container as a centerpiece for outdoor dining. People can pick the fresh leaves for sandwiches and salads.

Patio tomatoes are bred to excel in containers. They are stocky and may only need staking as fruit are ripening. Plant several two to three weeks apart to harvest container tomatoes all summer.

Radishes are one of the quickest crops in the garden. Smaller types can grow from seed to maturity in three and a half weeks. You can sow in succession and harvest continually from spring to frost. Or treat it as a cool-season crop and in summer use the container for beans or tomatoes.

Serviceberry 'Regent' is a small shrub that is suitable for container culture year-round. Sunny, dry, and windy areas, like balconies and roof decks, are just fine for 'Regent'. As a container plant on my balcony, it withstands both torrid summers and frigid winters that have killed many lesser shrubs. It is even salt tolerant. Clusters of white flowers cover the branch tips in spring. By June, the tasty berries are ripening in shades of red, blue, and deep violet.

Sweet potato vines trail to 6 feet or more and fill containers with lush leaves that cascade over the sides. While the edible sweet potato may not have the multicolored leaves of its ornamental siblings, they are just as decorative in form. Grow these in a large container and use the lush foliage as a backdrop for other containers. In fall, when night temps get below 55 degrees F, dig the tuberous roots from the pot.

BEST EDIBLE CONTAINER PLANTS

Plant	Container Size (minimum)	Container Conditions		
		Season	Shade Tolerant	Hardiness
Bush bean	20 in.	Summer	No	Tender
Chili pepper	12 in.	Summer	No	Tender
Kale	12 in	Spring to fall	No	Half hardy
Lemon thyme	12 in.	Spring to fall	No	Zones 3–9
Marjoram	12 in.	Summer to fall	No	Half hardy
Mizuna mustard	16 in.	Spring to fall	No	Half hardy
Patio tomato	6 in.	Summer	No	Tender
Radish	16 in.	Spring to fall	No	Half hardy
Serviceberry 'Regent'	20 in.	Summer	Yes	Zones 4–9
Sweet potato	20 in.	Fall	No	Tender

Best Management Practices

Best Management Practices (BMP) are a collection of techniques and methods used to grow healthy, productive plants. The practices are rooted in science and stress cleanliness. Best Management Practices also promote the conservation of resources, including water, time, and money. The practices include the following:

* Use clean tools and gloves when handling plants and crops. Diseases can spread by shovels, hand trowels, and other tools. Brush dirt off tools after every garden workday to keep them clean. If tools have been used on or near diseased plants, clean them with a 10 percent bleach solution.

* Clean pruners before using them on different plants. Spraying the blades with a 10 percent bleach solution prevents the spread of diseases. Make a pruning kit consisting of a spray bottle, bleach solution, and old towel so it is always handy.

* Maintain a healthy soil by amending with compost and organic matter. Your own compost is the best soil amendment. Composting recycles old leaves, stems, plant debris, food scraps, and grass clippings into nutrients that help feed and build soil.

* Maintain soil nutrient and pH levels at an optimal range. The best way to monitor nutrients and pH is to use soil test kits once every three years. Test in fall so you will have time to adjust the soil with amendments before the growing season.

* Maintain soil moisture at optimum levels for plant growth without wasting water. Water deeply and infrequently. For example, instead of watering 15 minutes every day, water for one hour twice a week. Watering deeply promotes deep roots, which improves the health of the plant. Limit water runoff from your garden. Water runoff moves nutrients out of your soil and into the local environment where they can cause harm to native habitats.

* Apply approved fertilizers so that nutrients are available when the crops need them. For example, apply fertilizer to tomato plants in spring so that nutrients are available for the growing seedlings. Do not add fertilizer to tomatoes in fall. Nutrients are not needed then, and the fertilizer will be wasted and possibly leached into the local environment.

* Rotate crops into different fields every season. This keeps pests and diseases from finding the same plant in the same place every year. It also keeps the crops from exhausting the same nutrients from the same plot or pot each year.

* Plant more than one type of crop (polyculture). Polyculture is insurance against crop failure. For example, if you grow tomatoes, plant other crops and herbs, but also plant more than one variety of tomato. Mix some cherry tomatoes with some standards and oxhearts to increase the diversity and lessen the chance of crop failure.

* Monitor for pests and use biological and mechanical means of pest control if possible. Check the undersides of leaves as you water or harvest. If you find pests, start with the most economical control method first: mechanical. Mechanical methods of pest control include handpicking, crushing, spraying off with the hose, and sucking up with a vacuum. Biological methods use good insects or bacteria to fight the bad ones. When you have to use chemical methods, follow directions closely. If possible, select a product approved for organic gardening.

USDA HARDINESS ZONE MAP

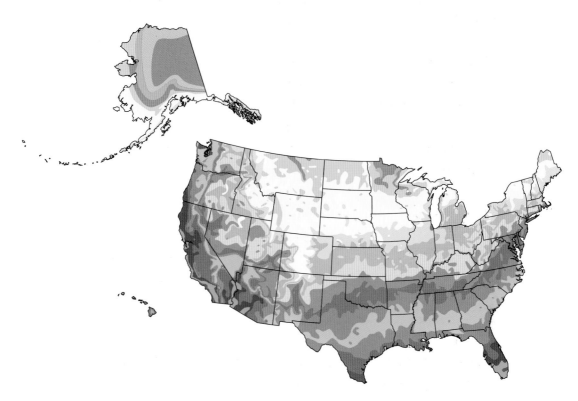

Average Annual Minimum Temperature

■	Zone 1, below -50	■	Zone 6b, 0 to -5
■	Zone 2a, -45 to -50	■	Zone 7a, 5 to 0
■	Zone 2b, -40 to -45	■	Zone 7b, 10 to 5
■	Zone 3a, -35 to -40	■	Zone 8a, 15 to 10
■	Zone 3b, -30 to -35	■	Zone 8b, 20 to 15
□	Zone 4a, -25 to -30	■	Zone 9a, 25 to 20
□	Zone 4b, -20 to -25	■	Zone 9b, 30 to 25
■	Zone 5a, -15 to -20	■	Zone 10a, 35 to 30
■	Zone 5b, -10 to -15	■	Zone 10b, 40 to 35
■	Zone 6a, -5 to -10	■	Zone 11, 40 and higher

GLOSSARY

Amend – to add materials to improve soil texture, drainage, pH, or fertility

Amendments – materials added to improve the soil

Annual – a category of plants that conclude their life cycle within one year

Best Management Practices (BMP) – standard horticultural practices that stress cleanliness and monitoring to increase yield while limiting costs and environmental degradation

Bulb – underground swollen plant stem, usually round, containing the following year's flower bud

Cat facing – irregular shapes and puckering on tomatoes caused by temperature fluctuations and incomplete pollination. This is a superficial condition that does not affect the taste.

Compost – decomposed kitchen scraps and plant debris

Ephemeral – annual or perennial with a very short season between emerging and dying back, typically wildflowers and bulbs

Evapotranspiration – the combined watering loss from evaporation and plant transpiration, which pulls water from the soil and releases it into the air

Flower – structure on plant used for sexual reproduction; contains sexual organs of the plant, usually colorful or fragrant to attract pollinators. If pollinated, it develops into a fruit.

Fruit – structure on plant that contains seeds, typically covered in pulp or flesh

Intercropping – planting different crops together

Interplanting – planting different plants together

Monoculture – large plantings of only one type of plant

Perennial – a category of plants that lives for more than three years

pH – measure of hydrogen ions in soil; determines availability of soil nutrients and minerals

Polyculture – large plantings of many different types of plants

Transpiration – the process by which plant roots pull water from the soil and release it into the air to quench their thirst and cool themselves

Tropicals – plants from tropical areas

Vermiculture – the use of worms to compost kitchen scraps and plant debris

Woody plant – perennials with woody branches, such as trees and shrubs

Meet William Moss

William Moss is a speaker, writer, and gardener, but most of all he is a teacher who inspires people to "Get Out & Grow." As a trusted authority on greening, gardening, and urban agriculture, Moss connects with audiences to explain how to make healthier choices to improve their lives, their communities, and their environment. Nicknamed the "Garden Boss" for his in-depth knowledge and sound advice, William uses his landscaping know-how and personality to engage, educate, and entertain audiences with relevant, informative content. His ability to bring complicated subject matter to life leaves audiences enthusiastic and charged.

William passionately spreads his love of the natural world. That love was fostered during his childhood in the foothills of South Carolina, and resurfaced years later in Chicago. After graduating from Northwestern University, William taught sixth grade. He later completed the Chicagoland Master Gardeners program and joined the Chicago Department of the Environment to work on habitat restoration and greening efforts throughout the city. This led to a career as a horticultural educator for the Chicago Botanic Garden, working with youth programs, adult continuing education courses, and school gardens.

William's ventures into television began with the Discovery Channel's *Rally Round the House* where he taught America about gardening, landscape construction, and plants. On TLC's *Town Haul* William designed artistic yet functional landscapes to get people outside and active. As host of HGTV's *DIG IN*, he helped homeowners tackle landscape projects resulting in dramatic transformations. William provided greening content for CBS's *The Early Show*, and appeared on QVC as a gardening guest.

William loves to spread the good news about gardening and greening. He writes content for various online, print, and social media including his website getoutandgrow.com. He serves on the advisory board for the urban agriculture venture, The Talking Farm, as spokesperson for the National Gardening Association, and as an instructor for the Chicago Botanic Garden. When he's not writing or producing videos, he is a landscape consultant and speaker.

William Moss lives and gardens in the Chicagoland area with his wife Natasha and family. This is his first book with Cool Springs Press.

INDEX

PHOTO CREDITS

Cool Springs Press would like to thank the following photographers and illustrators for their contributions to *Any Size, Anywhere Edible Gardening.* Unless otherwise noted, photography was supplied by author William Moss.

Jim Bashour: Pages 4 (top right, middle left, bottom left, bottom right), 6, 19, 21, 37 (right), 51, 53, 69, 132, 189

David Cavagnaro: Pages 119, 151

Heather Claus: Pages 22, 166

Thomas Eltzroth: Pages 79, 83, 87, 93, 105, 109, 123, 129, 184 (marjoram)

Katie Elzer-Peters: Pages 25, 27, 29, 30, 31, 32, 35, 37 (left), 38, 41, 63, 142, 154, 178 (carrot)

Greg Grant: Page 45

Mitch Lenet: Page 195 (bottom)

Paul Moore: Page 66

Natasha Moss: Page 194 (top left)

Shutterstock: Pages 16, 47 (left and right), 141, 161, 184 (serviceberry)

Lee Reich: Page 159 (top left)